"*Living Tidal* is a tc

a young woman who, pulled by the tug of romance and a desire to outdistance doubt, leaves family and familiarity to live on a sailboat in the open seas. Sheena Jeffers's story of adventure, romance, and transformation is lovingly evocative. This book speaks to anyone seeking the courage to plot a new course."

—Michael Paul Williams, Pulitzer Prize-winning columnist, *Richmond Times-Dispatch*

"More than just an adventure in paradise, *Living Tidal* is a journey in life, love, and self-discovery. This is a beautifully told page-turner."

—Neal Petersen, author, keynote speaker, sailor

"Part adventure tale, part love story, *Living Tidal* is a remarkable true tale which reminds us that sometimes, to restore wind to our sails, we need to try a different tack. This heartfelt, courageous memoir had me immersed in Jeffers's journey of self-discovery, tasting the salty sea, watching the constant moon, and rejoicing in the extraordinary act of being alive."

—Jill Witty, prizewinning author of *Witticisms*

"A wonderfully talented writer who combines raw, tender, dreamy, and unapologetic in her ability to untie the dock lines holding her back and trust the treasures that will alter her course in life."

—Darlene Kristi, world-traveling sailor and entrepreneur

"I felt like I was having tea with my best friend as I read Sheena's insightful and inspiring words. Her honesty and vulnerability connected with that voice we all have that asks the big life questions and wonders if we are on the right path. Learning to trust herself, mother nature, the universe, new friends, and even strangers, in *Living Tidal*, Sheena Jeffers gives the reader a wonderfully personal voyage of the mind, body, heart, and soul. It's a true 'coming-of-self' story that left me wanting more."

—Jessica Coffey, holistic living practitioner & advocate, world traveler

"Bravo! This authentic portrayal of the sailing lifestyle will encourage many dreamers to make the leap. Join Jeffers as she embarks on a heartfelt journey of self-discovery, leaving the familiar shores of her desk job and frozen dinners for the unknowns of life at sea with a new boyfriend. With vulnerability and humor, she shares her cruising experience in a way that captivates readers from start to finish. This is a truly enjoyable and entertaining read!"

—Fiona McGlynn, editor, WaterborneMag.com

"*Living Tidal* is a poignant, funny memoir that will resonate with everyone who has recognized a desperation for action and a frustration with their status quo. This book teaches you how to change your life."

—Kate Lewis, essayist with work featured in the *New York Times* and the *Washington Post*

"Hang around any boat ramp at the end of a holiday weekend and you'll witness how boatlife can challenge any relationship. So few people could live aboard—much less endure a catamaran crossing—while putting a young relationship to the test. Sheena Jeffers allows us to stow away on her intimate and sometimes heartbreaking odyssey through the Caribbean and Central and South America. This sensory journey is part memoir, part adventure, part romance. Tightly woven into the fabric of Sheena's journey are the women leaning into the wind as they offer kinship and service. From that first all-night radio conversation with a stranger, to the clicks of applause from a new community, to a couple seeking healthcare in a moment of dire need, to a mother and father's desparate plea—*Living Tidal* will stay with you, even when it's finally time to go home."

—Mary Franke, retired journalist and live-aboard boater

"This is a triumph! So tender and illuminating. A riveting journey of self-discovery. *Living Tidal* illuminates what is possible when you let go of fear and say 'yes' to adventure. Filled with heart, humor, and high-seas exploits, Jeffers's evocative prose made me feel like I was right there with her on the sailboat. Her story shows that sometimes you have to leave behind the life you know in order to find out who you really are and what you really want out of life."

—Olivia Campbell, *New York Times* bestselling author of *Women in White Coats: How the First Women Doctors Changed the World of Medicine*

LIVING TIDAL

SHEENA JEFFERS

BELLE ISLE BOOKS
www.belleislebooks.com

Excerpt from Mary Oliver's poem, "Wild Geese" printed with permission of Grove Atlantic, Inc. New York, NY

ISBN: 978-1-958754-84-9
Library of Congress Control Number: 2024902289

Designed by Sami Langston
Project managed by Jenny DeBell

Printed in the United States of America

Published by
Belle Isle Books (an imprint of Brandylane Publishers, Inc.)
5 S. 1st Street
Richmond, Virginia 23219

BELLE ISLE BOOKS
www.belleislebooks.com

belleislebooks.com | brandylanepublishers.com

For my children . . .

may you always know that adventure is possible right where you are.

U N I T E D S T

MEXICO

BEI

HO

GUATEMALA

EL SALVADOR

CO

Galapagos Island
(ECUADOR)

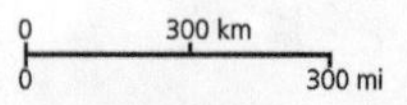

Norfolk, Virginia
Cape Lookout, North Carolina
Frying Pan Shoals
Charleston, South Carolina
Bermuda
(U.K.)
Fernandina Beach
Daytona Beach
New Smyrna Beach
Titusville
Vero Beach
West Palm Beach
THE BAHAMAS
Nassau
Thunderball Grotto
Key West, Florida
Georgetown
Turks and
Caicos Islands
(U.K.)
CUBA
Luperon
Samana
Puerto Rico
(U.S.)
Fajardo
St. John
Humacao
St. Thomas
St. Croix
Anguilla
(U.K.)
Cayman Islands
HAITI
DOMINICAN
REPUBLIC
ST. KITTS
AND NEVIS
JAMAICA
DOMINICA
ST. LUCIA
ST. VINCENT AND
THE GRENADINES
Aruba
(NETH.)
Aruba
Curaçao
(NETH.)
Bonaire
Curaçao
GRENADA
Cartagena, Colombia
PANAMA
San Blas Islands
Bocas del Toro
Panama Canal
Obladio, Panama
VENEZUELA
GUYANA
SUR.
COLOMBIA
ECUADOR
BRAZIL
PERU

Contents

Introduction

> *For a while we tramped on in silence, till Umbopa, who was marching in front, broke into a Zulu chant about how brave men, tired of life and the tameness of things, started off into a great wilderness to find new things or die. . . .*
>
> —H. Rider Haggard, *King Solomon's Mines*

All I could think about in 2016 was that something needed to change. I wished for a reset, a do-over—bigger even, a new me. But where does one sign up for less painful memories, a friendly and generous inner voice, more confident knowings? I didn't know where to begin until an opportunity appeared in the form of a forty-three-foot sailing vessel. This is the story of how a sailing vessel reorganized every part of me and life as I knew it. A boat, the open sea, our Earth's moon, and the teachers who appeared along the way transformed me from who I thought I was—a hapless victim—to a version of me who exists peacefully and confidently in who I am.

Sailing would have never occurred to me; that idea was reserved for storybooks, surly men of days long gone, billionaires, song writers, or artists with canvases. When the opportunity crash-landed into my life, it felt the way it'd feel if a UFO plowed into my backyard—foreign, messy, and inconvenient. It was my partner who—using tools of love, enthusiasm, and tireless dedication—showed me that the world opens to a heart daring to live expansively. For that, I'll always be grateful.

Anne Morrow Lindbergh wrote: "What are the accidents, the desires, the forces, one wants to know, that free him? . . . The man I was to marry believed in me and what I could do, and consequently, I found I could do more than I realized, even in that mysterious outer world that fascinated me but seemed unattainable. He opened the door to 'real life' and although it frightened me, it also beckoned. I had to go."[1] This is my story—as I remember it—of having to go. Of three gigantic life transformations that happened for me over the course of three years: 1) sailing away from the life I worked hard to build but struggled to enjoy, 2) learning to love and be loved, and 3) learning to love myself even more. The story of a gift I was given that altered the course and core of my being. The story of learning how to embody living tidal.

Limited to the confines of language, pages, and 104 keyboard keys, I couldn't possibly put everything here. Some memories I couldn't find the words for; they live in the spaces between the keys. The exact sailing course is altered here for brevity, with the removal of some quick stops and the intent to keep the focus on our main destinations. Some names of humans and vessels have been changed for privacy, most notably the vessel I sailed on and the partner I sailed with.

---

1. Anne Morrow Lindbergh, Hour of Gold, Hour of Lead (New York: The New American Library, Inc., 1973).

PART ONE

CHAPTER ONE

The Cosmic Boot

I faint, naked, while receiving my airbrushed tan. All 112 pounds of me blacks out.

My physical body buckles. *At least I'll be tanned,* I remember thinking as all went black.

For redheads, tanned skin is an inaccessible dream—off limits—denied. *Porcelain doll, translucent,* and *ghost* are words I identify with. My girlfriend invited me to join her family's vacation—a cruise, floating out at sea—so I need to cover up my embarrassing, pasty skin before wearing a swimsuit in public. It would be rude to foist paste upon others.

"Sheena? Sheena!" My vision slowly refocuses. I look around. Something got to me. Maybe it was the chemicals floating around in the small plastic tent or maybe something more insidious, but I am on the floor. The lady spraying my pale body caught me and has sat me up. "Have some wat—"

I throw up in a nearby trashcan. This tanning session is over.

I pour my half-tanned body into my car and make it to the highway. Traffic again. I shift my car into park on the interstate; the "70 mph" speed limit sign smirks. I think a lot of the same thoughts again—again and again. Today—again—it's *traffic—again.* Tomorrow—again—there will be traffic—again. I'll balance my coffee cup between my thighs as I unwrap my gas station blueberry muffin. My stomach will protest its black coffee coating. I'll think—again—traffic—*again.*

"What am I doing here?" I ask aloud—to no one. I often ask myself existential questions when I'm stuck in traffic, but mostly because I'm angry at myself for being stuck in traffic. *You should have listened to the radio traffic report—and not just with your ears but with some actual intent to heed the advice and take exit thirty-four before the backup.*

A horn blares.

"Really?" I yell, lifting my untanned arm while my tanned arm holds tight to the steering wheel. "Do you see the car in front of me *and* the car in front of that car and so on? Where exactly do you expect me to go?" The horn blower flips me off. My phone buzzes and I see the name of the guy I'm dating flash across the screen. His message:

"When do you get home? We should talk . . ."

The beep of my microwave snaps me back to the present. My frozen Lean Cuisine dinner—turkey, with a smattering of gravy, peas, and carrots, and a *sorry attempt* at mashed potatoes—is ready. Ten minutes earlier, I poked holes in the plastic and popped this baby into the microwave. He broke up with me.

"GIRL WHO CAN'T FIGURE LIFE OUT CREDITS MICROWAVED MEALS WITH KEEPING HER ALIVE"

Imagining newspaper headlines is a thing I do. It helps me keep everything real and focused, summing up my no-frills life in 280 characters or less. It's a skill engraved into me from college when I graduated with a degree in print journalism right as print journalism was closing up shop. I walked across the stage to accept my diploma in 2008 and wasn't even able to get it framed and leveled on a wall before newspapers started layoffs—reporters were sent dazed to their cars, carrying belongings in boxes asking, "What is Twitter anyway?" The housing market crashed three months later. But here I am, left with an unframed, un-hung degree and a skill of writing headline summations of my life circumstances.

I just don't want to be together anymore. This is what he told me. He said it wide-eyed and staring at me. He meant it.

I stir my half-warmed, half-icy mashed potatoes and replay the panicked storm of questions I asked following his revelation:

"But why?

"What went wrong?

"What did I do wrong, *exactly?*

He offered no answers.

"SINGLE GIRL STRUGGLES TO ACCEPT REALITY"

We said our goodbyes and I closed the door behind him. I watched my Lean Cuisine circle round and round and round and round in the microwave. I push the peas into the potatoes, creating "peas-in-craters" or "birds' nests" as I called them during my childhood. Feeling an awful lot like a bird tossed from its nest, I smoosh.

You just aren't relationship material, Sheena.

You aren't easy to love.

You'll never be someone's life partner.

You'll never get those "we're-so-in-love" photos. Much less a wedding.

You'll most likely be eating Lean Cuisines for a very, very long time.

When I was a small girl, I accompanied my mother to a veterinary appointment for our family dog who had been coughing wretched, labored coughs—fishhook-snagged-in-the-throat coughs. The vet came in holding a jar of alcohol in which floated a preserved heart eaten alive.

"Heartworms," he explained. I held the glass jar in my eight-year-old hand. My coughing dog sat patiently on her leash watching me turn the jar this way and that. Not a single part of the heart was left untouched by tiny worms. This was to be my dog's fate; it had already begun.

"Infested, the heart ceases to beat," the veterinarian said as he jotted down notes on our dog's chart. Most likely he wrote something like: "Sure to die soon."

I bite into a cold carrot twenty years after that vet appointment, wondering if *I* have heartworms. Self-deprecating thoughts nudge their way in like those tiny, abusive, life-threatening worms. I am choked, clogged. I cough up that cold chunk of carrot. My loveless, sexless future reeks of failed online dating, underpaid work, unending college debt, and having to accept that I will one day be a "woman of a certain age" who "missed her opportunity"—for everything. I throw the Lean Cuisine away. Some of it splatters on my floor, but I leave it and crawl into bed. *Fuck it.*

On weekdays, I work. With newspapers crumbling in 2008, I took a job as a legal assistant. They agreed to pay for my health insurance, plus I needed time to imagine up an entirely new life plan.

Within two years, I worked my way up from a cubicle to my own office—from assistant to paralegal—and, two years after that, I just couldn't do it anymore. I resigned and returned to graduate school to study my life's passion: dance. *This time I'd get it right*, I told myself. But after *that* graduation, which brings me to my life right now, I find myself in the same position: having to work to support dance. I take a full-time job as an arts integration director, which sounds fancy, but it is simply an admin role for a struggling nonprofit. Even with that job, I can't pay my bills, so I add three part-time jobs: two positions teaching dance; one teaching yoga. The exhaustion I feel is insistent. I'm not exhausted by the quantity of jobs. I'm exhausted by something far sneakier, something I can't touch or point to like an irregular-shaped mole or the precise location of a lingering headache. Having nothing to point to makes it difficult to express concern about my exhaustion to medical professionals. I'm exhausted because this isn't the life humans were designed for (*right?*), and I cannot make that ever-insistent thought go away.

"Is your coffee caramel?" My coworker bursts in. We're all wearing some version of the same outfit even though there isn't a dress code. Casual dress pants or *slacks*—for everyone. A blouse printed with florals or chic thin lines—for everyone. Ballet flats for comfort. For, of course, everyone.

"Yes," I confirm. I didn't want it to be caramel coffee, but that's all they had in the office basket of K-cups. "I was *wondering!"* she says, slapping her palm against her gym-membership-toned quadriceps. "All last week I couldn't figure out where that caramel smell was coming from." This search had really taken it out of her.

I nod my head and hold up my cup. "Guilty." My cup, stained and now cold, plops down on my desk, as exasperated as myself.

I love my coworker. She's fiercely intelligent, carries her Ph.D.-level complex thought everywhere she goes, and it's backed by a tireless go-getter attitude. She's particularly interested in female equality and empowerment (topics I would love to discuss with her) but coffee flavors and smells are the conversations we're forced to have—*forced* because it's made clear in the working world that you cannot be seen talking *too long* about anything *life-oriented* during *office time*. Such diversions are punishable as an abuse of *someone else's* time, time that is—quite simply—not our own. Interactions must be short, stiffened, and limited to surface-level inquiries so there is no risk of giving into the seductive forces of meaningful purpose.

Trivial conversations drain me. They eat away at me, corrode me. I become caustic in a matter of minutes. She walks away and I press my hands *hard* into my face, pulling downward. My muscles numb from the sheer blandness of it all.

I look at my work phone.

No calls.

I refresh my work e-mail.

No e-mails.

Why am I here again?

I look around to see if anyone else seems to feel as claustrophobic in these miserable circumstances as I. *No.* They like their jobs and their stability. They like their regular paychecks, their insurance, and their assuredness. They're *smiling?* I hold the space bar down on my computer and watch the cursor print blankness. *What is wrong with me? Why do I desire—obsess—over a different kind of freedom?*

These office scenes loop themselves. Each day I add a new layer of numb, whether it's from the air conditioning pumping out endless frigidity ("Please do not touch the thermostat," the sticky note reads), stale conversations with no expiration dates, meetings that leave my eyelids spazzing, or superiors who walk around believing everything is *just fine* ("Everything good?" they ask, with a thumbs-up). I leave at the end of each day covered in a metaphorical *gunk,* desperately wanting a shower. How dirty it feels to hold onto this emotional fury. How hopeless it feels to be stuck in it. Somewhere along the way I folded up my personhood into a paper airplane and tossed it aimlessly away. I'm left with the crash landing. I have betrayed myself by allowing someone else to decide, assign, monitor, evaluate, and declare my worth—my time's worth.

Five p.m. I sit in my car, which has warmed to over a hundred degrees in Virginia's humid summer heat. I wait until the coldness harbored in me dissipates. On my cheeks, my corporate-air-conditioned frostbite tingles as it transitions over to the summer scorch. I roll my neck around. The warmth slips down my neck, into my shoulder blades, through my arms and down to my fingers and toes. My core temperature rises, but the numbness remains. *Where can I go to escape this lack of feeling?*

Home. I shower, standing for too long under scalding hot water.

Still, nothing.

I stockpile soap in my palm and whirl it into a bubbled mess on my head. Then I carefully shape my hair into a cone-like sculpture while I shave my legs.

Nothing.

I let the water run over and down me and into the drain, wishing it could run straight through me.

Amazon search: "Soul-touching showerhead."

Wrapping a towel around my body, I pour a giant glass of white wine and gulp. *What are you doing? What are you going to do?*

My yearning for something other than this "real world" started off small and vague. It first showed up as tiny objections to unclear office organization, roles, and responsibilities. Then, it grew into an unspoken but constant fury I couldn't shake off. These gremlins manifested into eye rolls, deep sighs, and increased time spent at coffee, bathroom, and lunch breaks—micro insubordinations.

"Could display a more harmonious and cooperative spirit," my review paperwork reads. "But excels at meeting deadlines on creative tasks."

The process repeats itself at different jobs, within different teams of people, under different roles and responsibilities. Seed, germination, growth, reproduction, pollination, and dispersal: Such is the life cycle of my gremlins—manifestations of me yearning for something *more.* I've tried over and over again—as a freelance journalist, legal assistant, paralegal, dance professor, yoga teacher, and nonprofit director. I get paid to write answers for answers.com even though I don't have any answers. Something is wrong. The signs are here. This yearning-for-something-more malady is a trickster. It hops, skips, and jumps all over the place.

Depression?

Quite possibly.

Anxiety?

Check.

Restlessness?

Sure, some days.

Lack of passion?

For bullshit, sure. For living, no.

Complacency?

Unwanted, but yes, some of that.

I am a millennial working for baby boomers, which means a lot of looking at the same thing but seeing entirely different problems and solutions. They say there are no pills for unfulfilled yearning and desire.

"Pull yourself up by your bootstraps."

"This is just how the world works."

"You need tougher skin."

I am experiencing a *soul* problem, and Western medicine and therapy not only refuse to acknowledge that woo-woo mess, but simply can't—won't—help with anything unrelated to symptoms from bacteria, viruses, or diagnosable mental disorders. Insurance doesn't cover soul problems. Church is suggested.

It's important to note here that I keep most of my malaise to myself. To the public, I am thriving. I get my work done, on time, and I do it well. That work gets noticed, secures more funding, and momentum increases. I smile, keep going, pose for pictures, and schmooze potential funders. I win "Millennial on the Move" and find myself on the cover of a magazine. Externally, it's all *cheers!* and clinks of wine glasses. Internally, I'm flattened.

I take a day off from work and turn, in desperation, to Eastern-style healing. Back-to-back appointments are scheduled: acupuncture, massage, Reiki, and chiropractic care. I drop my body on table after table to be pricked, pounded, read, and popped.

Can you make me feel happy with my current circumstances? I ask with my body.

Can your needles release my growing irritation?

Can your hands move away this bad energy?

Can a different pressure adjust my attitudes?

A young acupuncturist, retired from ballet, asks, "What are you experiencing?"

I bite my lip, twiddle my fingers. *Suppression, I'm good at this.* There's nothing she can do. She's as powerless as I am, so I suppress my real answers which are:

Working in a field that isn't respected or funded enough to adequately survive. Check.

School debt crushing me. Check.

Bank systems suffocating me.

Deep-seated shame eating away at me.

Irritations chafing me.

Complex developmental trauma revealing itself to me. Check. Check. Check. Check.

Instead, I say, "A bit of neck tension. A sore piriformis muscle . . . and occasionally I feel frustrated with life." She bends down toward my ear and says, "I'm going to do a little something extra for your sadness."

I hadn't told her I was sad.

Standing in line at the bank, I flip through images on social media. Look how grown they are! Look how together they have it! Oh, would you look at that—solid, effective routines. So-and-so is expecting baby number three, and so-and-so got engaged. So-and-so just closed on their first—no wait—second home to be used for—you guessed it: summers!

I'm at the bank because I'm locked out of my account, *again*.

"Ma'am?"

"What? Hi, yes," I stammer, dropping back into reality.

"Shery can help you over here," the woman says, motioning with her arm and hand. I adjust my far-too-heavy bag—*Really, Sheena, what is in this bag*—and walk to the teller window.

"How can I help you today?" My banker is pretty. Curly brown hair falls onto the shoulders of her sharp, professional outfit. Her glasses fit her face just right. The name placard on the desk reads "Sherryl" but her name tag reads "Shery"—one *r*, not two.

"I keep getting locked out of my account. I think something is messed up in my online settings. My card got stolen a while back and they put extra protective—"

"Let's take a look," she says, cutting me off. She has the gist of it.

I swipe my card and she stares at her screen. "Oh. Mmm-hmm. OK, I see." Click around. Click around. Scroll. Click around. Mmmmm. Click.

"Are you aware your account has a negative balance?" she asks, eyeing me from the tops of her perfect glasses. I fidget.

"You know how it is: mortgage, paying off graduate school, bills, life!"

"OK, well, you know there *are* fees for that . . . ?" *Sherryl, God, yes. I know. Move on.*

She dives into a labyrinth of screens, makes a phone call to the IT department, and my settings are changed. "You shouldn't have any more problems. I've removed the high-security settings."

"Great!"

"You should really watch that account balance," she suggests, talking louder than necessary. "We can set up an alert for you if you'd like." *No, Sherryl-with-two-rr's. You just removed the alerts. I don't need an alert to remind me I'm drowning. That sounds delightful, but no.*

"No, thank you. I mean, it's not really a problem . . . most months." She doesn't believe me. She's seen my record. "Well, thank you for your help!" I walk out with a wave.

Unlocking my car, I return to that Virginia heat. It's one of my favorite things to do lately—just sit in the immense heat trapped in my car. I let it sink in deep. Let this sink in deep: nearly thirty years old. Broke. Single.

My phone buzzes. *So-and-so just received a promotion at work. So-and-so added an addition to their home. So-and-so completed their tenth marathon . . .* I toss it into the passenger seat. I was broken up with for vague reasons, a "just because" kind of thing, where the period is placed after the word "because" and nothing follows—*because nothing follows.* For some reason—more about my age and less about my love for this person—this breakup left me reeling. Those people in high school and college I thought would never get married *are* married, with children, homes, vacation homes, additions, promotions, and new cars. This isn't how I saw life playing out for them, and definitely not how I saw it playing out for me.

A knock at my car window.

"Hi," I hear a muffled voice say. I look through the window at a man wearing worn, tired, dirty clothes. I roll down the window just a bit, for safety, as my family always taught me.

"Any change?" I want to sit on the side of a curb with him and tell him how *little change* there is in my life. *No change, actually,* I imagine myself saying. I want to compare our brokenness—my looming college debt, monthly mortgage, electricity, and water bills. Twelve days until my next paycheck, and the "almost empty" yellow gas light stares at me. *Thanks, Sherryl, but I forgot to mention, I already have a low-balance alert installed in my goddamned dashboard.*

I wonder if he has any debt. I wonder how many times a bank has said to him, "I'm . . . I'm looking for a delicate way to put this." He may very well be better off than me, on paper and in life. Shit, at least the bank doesn't have an address of record to track him down to alert him of his low balance. I pass him the emergency toll money that I hide in my driver-side door. *Now I'm really broke.* "God bless," he says.

Yeah, dude. God. Bless.

I'm standing in line to order Chinese for one. A hand-scribbled sign reads: "Two packages of sauce per customer." I take only two packages even though everyone knows four is the perfect amount.

I am still waiting on my certificate from the Committee of Rule Followers. Inducted into the club at birth, I've remained an honest and active member—I use sick days at work only when I'm legitimately sick; I switch my cellphone to airplane mode *the moment* the flight attendant asks; I don't swallow bubble gum, and I wait thirty minutes after eating before swimming. I have followed rules for as long as I can remember. Growing up, I was mostly compliant, quiet, and tried to live without needs. I often tried to disappear entirely within the rules, so that all anyone could see was the rules I followed. As a child in elementary school, I wanted to purchase every preapproved item off my back-to-school lists *as specifically requested* by the school. I once corrected my mother when she held up something interesting but not on the preapproved list. "I know this isn't on your list, but this will be fine," she assured me.

"No," I replied, horrified. "I want exactly what they want me to have."

When I was a teenager, I never snuck out or disregarded my curfews. I never sipped alcohol until I was in college, where I served as a resident assistant and spent my time enforcing rules instead of toying with them.

Now I'm starting to feel intolerable rage around "the good girl" parts of me. What has she brought me?

Expectation 1: Achieve good grades in school. *Check!*

Expectation 2: Be kind, fair, genuine, and a good Christian. *Check!*

Expectation 3: Attend and graduate college with good grades. *Check!*

Expectation 4: Secure a good-paying job that offers benefits and health insurance. *Check!*

Expectation 5: Remain in said job by performing well and receiving annual raises. *Check!*

The good girl breezed through those expectations, and she was "on-track" in life.

But what it took of me to achieve those expectations has led me here: angry, full of dread and self-doubt. Perfectionistic striving with little to no self-worth, wandering around a world with a menacing cloud over me. Why couldn't the expectations be: Choose happy. Choose healthy. Choose adventure!

Back at home, my hamster cheeks packed with chicken and broccoli, I scribble out a resignation letter to the Rule-Following Committee on the back of a napkin.

To whom it may concern,

I have followed the rules expected of me for three decades. Those rules provided me structure, safety, and clarity when navigating new territories such as childhood, puberty, and adulthood. I've made it through without becoming an addict or unexpectedly pregnant and without a prison record or shredded credit score. However, my time in this lively club has come to an end. I appreciate the lessons you've taught me, but I choose to leave these lessons here and practice a different kind of boldness, curiosity, assertiveness, and creativity instead. I will try "making my own rules" from here on out.

Please accept this letter as my resignation and declaration that I am leaving this position to move onward to rules and expectations set by me, for me.

With appreciation,
The Good Girl

I trace over the words "I choose."

I choose.

Having no one to submit my resignation letter to, I crumple up the napkin and throw it in the trash. I fish it back out just before I head to bed and lean it against my coffee pot.

I choose.

CHAPTER TWO

GIRL MEETS FUTURE

Two years pass, and I'm not sure I notice. I buy new pants for work and spend my bachelorette hours eating frozen foods or ordering small pizzas and never finishing them. I dance at weddings by myself and wrap countless baby shower gifts only to have to say, "Oh, no; I'm single. No babies in my immediate future," a hundred times while stuffing pink or blue or yellow pastries in my mouth. I try to explain, "I *also* don't know why I'm single" with hamster cheeks. My singleness, while fun and productive at some points, is starting to rub me the wrong way.

"It'd be nice to have someone who notices if I don't make it home safely at night—" I tell my girlfriend at work one day, "—or know that someone would want to help if I'm choking on a grape." My friend sets me up on a date out of legitimate concern: she's seen the size of the grapes I pack for lunches. A guy from the internet wants to meet me, she says.

Name: Kallan

Picture: attractive

Work: real estate agent

—along with phone number, location, and time of our meeting. It's scheduled for a Tuesday night. Nothing too sexy happens on a Tuesday night so it doesn't feel too serious.

Date night arrives and I'm coming straight from my part-time gig of teaching ballet to pre-teens. My hair is in a bun—not the cute kind you see pulled into sloppy perfection, but a genuinely unwashed bun packed full of oil and sweat. I'm wearing black yoga pants and a leotard, which I cover with a button-up jean shirt. Remnants of makeup remain, but sweat washed three-quarters of it off hours ago. One eye is outlined and the other not so much. It'll do.

I make a right turn into the restaurant parking lot, and he is standing outside. Wavy, ruffled, brown hair with sun-touched tips falls into his hazel eyes; completely acceptable for a beach-living guy and it completely works on me. He waves to get my attention, and I'm thankful to have that first awkward moment of "Is it you I'm meeting here?" over with. His shirt is just tight enough and with the correct number of buttons undone so I can see his muscles chiseled by surf trips; the breeze off the Chesapeake Bay lifts the flappy ends for torso peeks.

All the obvious parking spots are full. It's summer in our beach town of Virginia Beach, Virginia, but the good girl in me wants a spot that is clearly marked: two white lines with adequate space for a Hyundai Elantra. No spaces appear.

Noticing my distress, he walks over to me, and I roll the window down.

"Do you think this is a parking spot?" I ask. These are the first super-cool words I say to him. This space is open land. No markers grant approval to park there, but no markers forbid it, so it's up to me to decide. I shirk off the invitation to decide for myself—I'd rather be told. He looks at the open land.

"Sure!" he says, shrugging his shoulders, his breath smelling of the cigarette he just tossed. "Make it one."

M*ake it one? You can't just claim space as your own. Make it one!?* The smile in his eyes intrigues me.

I shift my car into park—making it one—and, silently, hope it will be there when I return. Internet-stranger Kallan stands unperturbed—not a single appearance of worry marks his face or body. If he's daring me with those eyes and that smile and that hair, I'll take the bait. I turn off my car and step out.

"Hi," he says, obviously proud of my cavalier parking. I smile back. I'm proud of myself too. We find two bar stools and a bartender. A cheap beer and a glass of Pinot Grigio appear, and the bartender returns to refilling the already-filled nut bowls and wiping down counters that are already spotless.

On first impression, the guy across from me is charming in a confident and carefree way. He moves in close to me at all the right times, touching my arm, leaving a chill from his beer-cold fingers. He laughs. He pushes his hair from his eyes. He's active. He's all over the place yet concentrated on me. I'm charmed by his reactions to my stories: "No way. Tell me more," he says, hungry to hear more. And I spill more.

I wonder his first impression of me: generally happy with a side of unspoken angst; an energetic spirit with a good-enough body, brimming with an undecided sense of purpose. A redhead, talkative, funny even; blue eyes, freckles, and full of stories—

"I want to sail around the world." He says this as easily as he tells me his astrological sign (Leo) and sets his beer down. Then he leans back, arms crossed as if so much hinges on my next reaction. There's his smile, the squinted eyes, the baited silence. We're playing no-limit Texas Hold 'em and he's waiting to see if I'll ante up. I swallow my gulp of wine.

"Oh yeah?" I scoot to the edge of my chair, holding his eye contact. "That would be fun." Romantic images of a sun-kissed me in a string bikini sipping a cocktail roll through my head; it's intoxicating. But it's impossible. I can't tan, remember? I have jobs and debt. So, no, I close down the idea in my head. When I hear people mention their grandiose dreams, I file those conversations in the "If I ever win the lottery" category of my mind. Sure, you'll sail around the world. Sure, I'll win the lottery.

But he speaks with informed passion—rapid-fire—a conductor enamored by his own orchestra. He knows how to make this dream happen. His credentials come pouring out:

He's lived on a boat before.

He lived in St. Croix (with an ex-wife, but he breezes over that).

He worked on charter boats.

He's a licensed boat captain.

He sailed from St. Croix back to Virginia, where he was struck by lightning—*boom!* Lost all engine power but, *shiver me timbers*, he's innovative and docked that boat safely back at home.

My eyebrows raise at every credential he ticks off. But no, no, no, no. Credentials don't make dreams happen, I tell myself.

"Another glass?" The bartender asks, smiling. I wonder if this same bartender has watched Kallan have this same conversation with other women. Kallan looks at the bartender and back at me: "Hot tub instead?"

Back at his house, I'm pulling one of his T-shirts over my oily hair, body, and panties and stepping into his hot tub.

"GIRL MEETS PIRATE ON THE INTERNET: INITIAL PARLAY SET"

"So," my girlfriend asks the next day at work, nudging her elbow into my rib.

"We're definitely going to date," I confess. I turn my computer on, blushing.

"I knew it."

A few weeks of whirlwind romance later, I come up for air. I respond to a "Hellooooo, Earth to Sheena" text from a girlfriend. I agree to meet her for brunch and peel myself from his side. She's wearing her new tortoiseshell glasses and we're eating overpriced French toast with truffle butter.

"You're alive, I see." She doubles down on the syrup. I spill to her that I've been living in a haze of let's-meet-up text messages involving kisses that taste of summer and sunscreen; bicycle rides along the boardwalk; popping open crab shells for the sweet meat; Hobie Cat sails; calling out of work—for the first time in my life—by *claiming* illness though I'm perfectly well. Instead, we'd head for spontaneous surf trips to the Outer Banks where I'd watch Kallan get barreled by waves. The good girl in me would have never taken so many liberties, or been able to enjoy them. But she's loosening up as days speed by. I haven't needed long showers in an effort to not feel numb anymore. Adventure is only ever a text away. My girlfriend is impressed—less by the adventures and more with her blossoming friend sitting across from her.

"Still," I confess, reeling myself back in, the conservative and previously-broken-up-with parts of me wonder: "Too much too fast? Maybe I should slow it down?"

"Listen," she says, "I met my now-husband while drunk on a dance floor at a club. Not the best marriage qualifications for either of us. And we built a beautiful life together! The thing is, sometimes you just have to do it. You just have to say, 'OK, sure! I'll go with the flow here. I'll move in with you and we will do this life thing—together.'"

She and I both know what the problem is: I'm not a "just do it" girl. And I think about that without saying it as I wiggle the outside edge of my fork through my goldened French toast. Occasionally I've flirted with the idea of being a "just do it" girl. I accelerated through a yellow light that turned red on me when I really should have stopped. I peed on a bush in a nationally protected park. I drank a little wine after taking Advil—once. I even went an extra thirty minutes past the designated time to reapply my sunscreen. Other than that, I'm still more of a research-based, pro-and-con-weighing, scientific-method-testing, rule-following girl. And, if we're looking at the facts here, no other relationship for me—zero—has ever worked out. Could I change this truth about myself? Could I adapt and become someone with a more carefree spirit? Be the girl who just moves in with the guy? The girl who makes a parking spot a parking spot just because I say so?

I like this guy, and he feels like a lot to me. When you've lived a life locked into schedules, systems and limiting beliefs, any sense of spontaneity will feel threatening. My thoughts vacillate between accusatory and curious. How dare he live so free . . . but this feels nice . . . .

Kallan is the storm I never saw coming. The storm I need to effectively drive out erosion of everything not working in my life. The exciting kind of storm that rushes in on a hot summer day to cool everything down, scattering beachgoers and flipping umbrellas inside out. A reorganization of sorts, and afterwards, the temperatures are cooled, the blue skies return, and beachgoers move on with their happy day; the whole scene leaves everyone refreshed. Kallan refreshes me daily, and I can't pin down how or why, which intrigues me and challenges me. When he speaks, he bypasses the scared, insecure good girl and talks directly to someone else within me. Who is she? Why don't I know her better? I'm suddenly a psychologist, a detective—any role I can take on to figure this out: how can anyone be so carefree? Who is this person he thinks I am? I am given confidence, spontaneity, practically a new character, it seems. My searches only return this fact: I am in love.

***

The prude in me surrenders a month into our escapades, and I agree to stay the night with him—the whole night, not a 3 a.m. exit while adjusting my top. I am breaking all of my rules—*wait. Are they mine? Or someone else's for me?* Whatever they are, I'm loving breaking them and the night fades into a steamy haze. I am both in time and removed from it. The next morning, he appears in his robe with a cup of coffee and a newspaper.

"Good morning," he says, in his cheery, soothing voice. "I want you to have a slow and calm morning." I pull my fingertips he's kissing from his soft lips and inch deeper into the sea of blankets and pillows. "Yeah. You enjoy," he says in his alarm-free voice, tying his robe a little tighter.

"Here is a cup of coffee for you, and the newspaper." I'm smiling. I'm impressed. *He would care if I choked on a grape.* "Your car was broken into last night and the police are here, but don't worry. I'll handle it."

"What?" *Full stop.* "*My car* was broken into? The police are here?" *What?* I'm throwing the blankets off my body. I don't know if I'm saying "what" to the fact that my car was broken into or reacting to *how freaking calm* he is about the fact that my car was broken into. *Why aren't we running downstairs?* I get up and rush around. *How did my bra get there?*

Kallan heads *slowly* downstairs to speak with the cops. *This is probably—definitely—a red flag (right?),* I think to myself as I scramble to line my boobs up with triangle bra cups. My first night—my *first* night—spending the night with him and there is broken glass everywhere and the police are involved? *See, Sheena. The one time you break your rules—trying to "live free"—this is what you get.*

I find Kallan outside in his robe with the police, leaning his elbow on the cop's window and smiling, a breezy position for his undercarriage. I can tell he is enjoying it—his coffee in one hand, talking in a low voice as if they were high school buddies discussing a ball game. I make my way to them, shattered glass snapping under my shoes. My leather bag with my iPad, my journal, and my calendar—gone. A giant rock sits heavy in the torn upholstery of the driver's seat. When Kallan sees me come outside, he doesn't even change his demeanor. He just smiles and welcomes me in.

"This is the lovely owner of the vehicle."

"Good morning, ma'am," a young, sleepy cop says. I learn that he is coming off shift and this is to be his last report before making his way to bed as the sun comes up.

"Can you tell me what you're missing?" I take a careful look and start listing the missing items. The cop flips his small notebook closed way too soon. Way too soon. I might have more to say. "Listen, ma'am. This guy really likes you," he starts. *What?* I find myself, again, unsure if I'm asking myself "what" because I'm shocked by the lack of professionalism or if I'm surprised Kallan likes me enough to tell this stranger. The cop continues, "Look at the guy; he enjoys your company," the cop says, motioning to Kallan standing in his robe, drinking his coffee. He lifts the cup as if to say, "Cheers, old sport!"

"OK, well . . ." I say, turning back to the cop trying to reinstitute some kind of professionalism into this interaction. "Is it possible to get my stuff back?"

"Most likely, no. Do you have the serial number of the iPad? We'll do some asking around, but it's most likely gone," he says. Since *no normal human being* carries around the serial numbers of their technology with them, I thank him for his time and slink back into the house. Kallan gives me a big hug and apologizes for the situation.

"I'll get you a new iPad," he whispers to me. And he does.

Two weeks later, we're driving down the road eating strawberries he picked up at a stand—farm dirt and all—when he says, "I like spending time with you. Will you be my official girlfriend?"

"Yes!" without hesitating. Then I turn away from him to look out of the window and smile. Butterflies, not worms, fill my heart.

Two months later, we're riding bicycles along the oceanfront when Kallan's effervescent love conjures up the desire to hold my hand while we're riding. His confident coordination can handle it. My jittery anxiety sends my bike careening into a bush. I break an arm that he helps me tenderly stabilize all the way to the doctor. I don't mind much. I am falling hard for this adventurous, big-hearted lover. Adventure and risk come with the unknown—but they're considerably less soul numbing than guard-walling them from your life altogether.

We give to our relationship—sun, water, nourishment, and, like a tropical plant, it flourishes. We attend a wedding together. We meet each other's parents. We move through our first disagreement with an ease that surprises me. I laugh more than I worry, an entirely new concept for me.

And then a FaceTime call comes in while I'm at work. I scurry off to the bathroom to take it. It's Kallan with excitement visible all over his face. He is electrified. He's breathlessly walking down a dock.

"I found the boat," he says. "She's a world traveler." I knew Kallan had been searching for boats, and I hadn't forgotten his "I want to sail" dream. I just hadn't given it any fuel for the flame because who wants to be reminded that a dream isn't working out? He turns the camera so I can see the boat.

"Isn't she great?"

"Oh . . ." I say, unsure of what I am actually seeing. "Yeah . . . she's floating!" I motion to my coworker and mouth the words, "I just need to finish this call" as she's washing her hands.

Kallan hops aboard and gives me a video tour of an extremely dirty, very broken boat. Cushions stained. Paper peeling. Mold accumulating. All of the important navigation technology stripped. None of that comes close to dampening his excitement. He must have a vision I am unable to see. I get the general gist though: two sleeping quarters, a kitchen, a pantry, two bathrooms with showers, and an office—all currently above water. He's listing other features I know nothing about, like solar panels, water tanks, foot pumps, wind vanes, and an autopilot.

"None of them work right now, but they will."

It's fun to watch people you care about feel jazzed by opportunity even if it's impossible to grasp that excitement yourself. My infatuation with him matches his infatuation for the boat, and the next day, he is ready to show me in person.

We drive to the marina, arms stretched out of the windows, hands sliding through the speeding summer air. When we arrive at the marina, another person is there viewing the boat, too. The broker welcomes us aboard.

The other prospective buyer surfaces from down in the cabin.

"It's a nice boat," he says, wiping dust from his hands onto his pants, "but it has too many problems. It'll cost a fortune and a lifetime to fix this thing. The wife would kill me." He walks off. The broker and I glance over to see if that reality had punctured Kallan. Nope. Hearts spill from his eyes. He is madly in love, inflated with hope.

I feel removed from it all. I'm not Kallan's wife, so I don't get an opinion. Besides, it's not going to touch *my* finances so that's not an issue. What harm is there in having a weekend hobby? I wonder who he needs me to be here? I am here to be . . . what exactly? Eye candy? Support? A girlfriend? An encouraging voice? A set of completely-uninformed-about-sailboats eyes? An unacquainted sounding board? I figure it doesn't matter labeling who or what I am at this point. I want to be here to see this joy.

We finish up our tour, and Kallan is shaking hands with the broker. Nobody knows it at this time (except for Kallan, who knows deep down this boat is his), but I am standing on the boat that would become my future home. Back in the car with seatbelts fastened, he looks at me matter-of-factly.

"That's going to be our boat."

Our? Did he just say, "our"?

"I'm putting in a bid."

"BOY WHO CAN ONLY SEE ROSES BUYS A DARK STORM CLOUD"

The broker receives four other, full price, sight-unseen offers—one from France and three from the States, all of which are contingent on a survey. This is when everything speeds up.

"I called the broker and told him this is meant to be my boat. I told him—" Kallan takes a deep breath and continues "—I have seen the fire damage. I see the fiberglass-damaged hull, and the broken daggerboards. I know the systems have been stripped away, and I realize I am only seeing ten percent of the work that will be required. The batteries are dead, and any survey on this boat will come back inconclusive because you can't test systems without power. The other buyers will bail when they see the amount of inestimable work." Another breath and he continues, "I told him I will get a high-interest loan and produce cash. My offer will not be contingent on a survey. I will close in a week and get this beat-up boat off your books. I'm offering sixteen thousand less than you're asking, but of all the offers you have, I will be the only one who will close. I told the broker that everyone else who puts in a bid will treat her like a weekend boat. Not me. I will live here. I will sail her around the world. She is my dream."

Then things go silent. The world around him, the world around me, the world around us. We await a decision—will the broker choose him?

Days pass. I wonder what is going on with the boat deal but don't ask. If he doesn't get chosen, I know he'll be devastated, and I prepare myself for a role I haven't yet played as his girlfriend—helping someone you care for through resounding disappointment.

Then the call. "I got the boat!"

Kallan's life transforms the second the keys are in his hand. Here is his life's new floating focus. Now every conversation we have revolves around *how*: how to pay off, to repair, to move onto, to live in and sail this vessel; how to thrive, to enjoy, to discover, to embrace the pinnacle of living on this vessel.

***

When a dream becomes reality, the weight of reality eventually seeps its way into the dream. Kallan starts to hear the ticking of the bomb he's standing on. He got the high-interest loan, so now the pressure is on—

. . . to sell his home,

. . . pay off the loan,

. . . then pay off the boat,

. . . and get working on repairs before winter weather and shorter days come.

With the pressure of it all, Kallan and I begin to fight. Not the romantic "Oh, we had our first disagreement—how cute—now, let's make up" kind of fight. No, we bubble over with stress and let it out on each other in harsh, childlike ways, a drastic change from our usual dreamy affairs. One particular fight brought everything to a head.

It was at the end of a long day for the both of us. He's covered in sweat and boat oil. I'm uptight from a board meeting that ran overtime and still solved nothing. We met in the kitchen, both of us irascible.

"We don't have to go to the boat *every* day," I point out.

"I want to be there every day. I come home from the boat just for you, otherwise I'd be sleeping there too."

"The boat isn't ready for sleeping."

"Yes, it is. You just sleep on it."

"OK. Between our jobs and boat work, and you *sleeping* on the boat, when do we have anytime together? And what about selling your home? And also, we can't leave our jobs, our lives, and our families just because you bought a stupid boat."

Silence.

I didn't mean to call his dream a stupid boat.

I fall into one of the wicker chairs in his kitchen as he stares, in the loudening silence, into his refrigerator. We both know that what he is looking for isn't in that refrigerator. He is looking for me to be one hundred percent on board with "The Boat" and everything that comes with it—

... the time and effort the project requires,

... the belief and confidence in his sailing dream,

... the adventurous, hopeful, dedicated spirit you must become to not give up on it.

He is looking for me to be positive and to "trust in the unknown" to take care of everything, and to take care of us. I am, as we are both starting to realize, none of those things—especially not on a consistent, dependable basis. I don't know how to be *that* bold and adventurous (especially not on my measly budget), and I definitely don't know how to trust something as vague as *the universe* to pay my monthly bills. He is asking me to have faith in the unseen, and that doesn't sit well next to nearly expired milk and yogurt, or whatever he is actually looking for in the refrigerator. When he breaks the silence, he does so with what sounds like a crack in the earth.

"I'm doing this with or without you," he says. We both know he had to say that. I know he wishes he didn't have to.

I understand his dilemma more than I am willing to admit. I had recently placed Paulo Coelho's *The Alchemist* into my Amazon cart and it arrived "nearly new—barely used" on my front door a month before Kallan's declaration. I spent one week reading all about personal legends and how the universe will conspire to help you on your path *once you're on it.* According to Coehlo, a personal legend is a destiny propelling a person toward what was always intended for them; to ignore a personal legend could lead to ruin. Reading the book was a lot like taking an existential multivitamin—full of everything I needed to hear but most of it I would most likely pee out, my body not understanding how to absorb it. I know this sailing adventure is Kallan's personal legend, and watching him so intentionally build it with each nut and bolt he purchases, fills me with ... jealousy? *Where is my personal legend?* Or how about tantrums? *Why is the boat more important than our relationship?* Imposter syndrome? *I don't deserve a personal legend such as this.* Fear? *He's doing this with or without me.* Doubt? *He won't want to stay with me.*

I'm not sure what I'm filled with, but I know it all feels heavy and negative. I can't find the excitement he lives on. I can't see that, maybe, his personal legend is an invitation to practice trusting that the universe will conspire to help *me* too—once I become brave enough to start down the path.

We stand looking at *Seas Hope*. That is to be her new name, he announced one day. "*Seas Hope*, because that's the key to life: believing it, seeing it, noticing it, then taking action." I love this about Kallan. His spirit is intoxicatingly motivating. "Does it look like she's . . . leaning?" Kallan asks. I tilt my head toward my left shoulder and nod.

"Oh, yeah . . . she's leaning." Since she's a catamaran, she has two parallel hulls, and her port side is taking on water, resulting in a significant tilt.

While dining one night at a local marina, a guy beers-deep into his evening strikes up a conversation. He scoots into the booth with us, covering his mouth to catch an escapee hiccup.

"Are you the couple who bought the Catana 431?" Then words fly out of his mouth for over an hour. We sit wide-eyed as we pop popcorn shrimp into our mouths, listening to new-to-us information that everyone in our small coastal town seemed to already know: The previous owner had dismasted[2] the vessel not once but *three times*. Once, he had entered waypoints into the GPS and fallen asleep—the boat steered straight into a bridge. The impact woke him from his drug-induced slumber down below. The second time, he was pushing the boat too fast in too high of wind. "He damn well knew he should've reefed." The third time? No one really knows what happened, "but it happened," they say.

There were tales of a wealthy ex-wife swimming in family money who, on a romantic high, financed the boat to be made and delivered from France—new—for her love. But after their relationship soured, she left him and the boat mortgage with a flip of her hair. While awaiting the inevitable bank reclamation of the vessel, he pushed the boat beyond her limits, and out of fury

2. To break off the tall upright post of the vessel

toward bankers, stole or broke anything he could before she was repossessed. A growing gloom rises in me as similar stories emerge from the sailing community—stories here and there, from this person, then that. *Is it possible to have mold in your stomach? Can humans have heartworms?*

"I wouldn't touch that boat with a ten-foot pole."

"Oh yeah, I remember that guy. I remember that boat. Good luck."

"I'm surprised that boat is still floating."

Kallan is silent on the drive home from dinner. I thought—possibly—some of these stories had gotten to him; he would see—possibly—that this is all insanity. But none of this information seems to have fazed him in the slightest. He isn't silent from fear; he is silent with even more focused determination to succeed.

I am shaken. He is in love. I am deflated. He is motivated. I see a problem and he sees an opportunity. I so badly want to see what he sees—for his sake; for our relationship's sake. How can two people look at the same thing and see such different realities? The answer is experience. The answer is faith. He sees through eyes of faith grounded in experience. I see through eyes of doubt and fear. We stop at a traffic light. I can see what he is thinking: *The boat hasn't sunk, yet, which means there is hope. There is time.* But *Seas Hope* needs to come out of the water *soon*.

The next day Kallan tows *Seas Hope* from Norfolk to Cape Charles, Virginia, and lifts her from the water. She's now safe. "On the hard," the sailors say. She's ready to become unbroken, and she'll stay here for months until she's floating confidently again.

I try to wrap my head around the kind of person who does this: buys a broken boat and believes—without an ounce of doubt—it will float! Safely travel the open ocean! The kind of person who leaves—without hesitation or guilt—the life, I thought, humans were compelled to live. I hadn't realized yet that "the life" I believed was the *only* option, was just that: an option. Among *other* options!

Kallan tracks down the original owner when he stumbles upon an advertisement posted by the man on Craigslist. The ad lists every missing part from our boat. "It has to be him," Kallan says. So, Kallan calls the number listed on the ad and disarms him enough to eke out a confession: He stole them hoping to resell them because, "fuck banks," he told Kallan on the phone. I receive a text from him: "Found the original owner. I'm going to negotiate a price to get our stuff back."

Kallan pulls up to a dilapidated home where the man is obviously squatting—no running water or electricity in sight. Parts of our boat are strung about, hanging over tree branches and splayed out on the floor of the garage—guts he yanked out of our boat that we need. He is charging "non-negotiable" 2016 prices for 1998 boat parts. "I have bills to pay," he says, while cracking open a beer. Kallan refuses to buy anything at the prices he's demanding and leaves.

This all happens while I am at work—with mold in my stomach.

***

On TV, the newscasters are agitated. Their voices elevate and their eyes open wide as they point to the red blotch splashed across the screen. Hurricane Matthew is a Category 5 storm with seventy-five mph wind gusts—and headed straight for our hometown of Norfolk, Virginia, a waterfront city at the southeastern base of the Chesapeake Bay that is prone to major flooding.

"Take this hurricane seriously," the meteorologist says. Kallan and I glance at each other. We need Jimmy.

Not long after buying the boat, Kallan befriended a boat captain, Captain Jimmy, who was living, unexpectedly, on his boat just up the street from Kallan's home.

"He's having troubles at home," Kallan explained to me one day as we flipped burgers over on sizzling-hot racks.

Kallan turns his eyes away from the screen alerting us of oncoming destruction. "I told Jimmy he could stay with us during the hurricane—" he spills, followed by, "—he can't stay on his boat!" "With us," means "at Kallan's house." I bounce between my beach condominium and Kallan's house, but since he owns a hot tub, when I debate where I want to stay, his house often wins.

When I first heard about Captain Jimmy, I advocated hard against him living with us, mostly on the basis that he was a stranger. Kallan fought for him because he trusts that the universe provides helpful opportunities. He laid out his logic: we could charge him rent and we need all the extra cash we can get for boat repairs. Having glimpsed the price tag on a single stainless screw at West Marine, this was a valid point. And now, eyeing the TV with the blotch moving closer and closer, I acquiesce. We need Captain Jimmy because I sure as hell don't know how to protect *Seas Hope*—that we just put back in the water after months of being dry docked—during a Cat-5 hurricane, and I don't want her to sink. We're trying to save an uninsured sailboat Kallan just bought on credit and Jimmy can help.

Kallan calls with the official "come on over; it's getting bad out there." Captain Jimmy arrives with a single plastic garbage bag of clothes. He is older than we are by thirty years, a father of two children about our age. This is all I know of him. I side-eye him over my steaming coffee. Who is this random boat-dweller? Why should I trust him? No one brings a complete stranger over to their home to live for a while. Has Kallan never seen a murder documentary? Because this is how they start!

"Nice to meet you," he says, not unlike a serial killer. But, as I'm showing him to his bedroom, I realize that I don't actually know how a serial killer would say that.

We hunker down for the storm at Kallan's house with the intention to visit the marina every half hour, or as needed. Captain Jimmy makes multiple trips with us to the marina to help keep an eye on our new boat. When the storm surge rushes in, lifting her parallel hulls even with the pier, we worry the wind will throw her straight into the concrete, piercing her hulls. Captain Jimmy throws on his foul-weather gear and kicks open the car door, struggling headfirst against pelting rain in order to spiderweb lines that will hold the boat in place.

Maybe he's a good guy?

Back at Kallan's house, seeking reprieve between marina trips, we sit around the fire with hot chocolate and listen attentively for any shifts of wind. A shift requires us to repeat the process: put on foul-weather gear, head out into the rain, retie the lines. Captain Jimmy does this every time without the slightest complaint. In fact, there's such a professionalism about his approach that Kallan and I soak up all of the wisdom he's yelling over the speeding winds. He's impressive, there's no doubt about it. The storm passes and the sun returns, drying up water sitting in ditches and yards. Jimmy stays with us for longer than the storm because, well, he's won us both over. For everyone's planning, we needed to come to a formal decision: Is Captain Jimmy our formal roommate?

"He's a good guy, right? You like him?" Kallan asks, stirring sugar into his coffee. He whispers because Captain Jimmy is still asleep upstairs. "If you want him to go, I'll tell him to go, but he's been very helpful. . . ."

He isn't wrong. Jimmy knows we're working on two major projects: the boat and selling the house. He's helping with both, which we need, plus I haven't noticed anything odd or alarming about this Captain Jimmy character. Is it possible that the universe sends you a stranger who isn't . . . dangerous? That night, I was jokingly complaining to Kallan that he hasn't taken me on any dates lately.

"I took you whale watching."

"That was a month ago," Jimmy interjects, not moving an inch; his face still buried in whatever newspaper he is reading, and his crossed legs haven't adjusted a bit. He's just a man in a corner spitting out facts.

"See!" I say, trying not to laugh. It feels nice to have someone support you, regardless of how well you know them. "I appreciate you noticing that, Jimmy," Kallan says, an obvious eye-roll in his tone. While we're on our date, Jimmy formally moves in.

The high-interest loan Kallan took out to purchase the boat has left him balancing two mortgages, and he is starting to feel the pressure of that financial responsibility with each passing day. *Seas Hope* was purchased with the intent of living on her full-time, which means his house must be sold in order to plow that money into paying off the boat loan—leaving him with zero mortgages. Here I am, a relatively new girlfriend still trying to get to know my relatively new boyfriend, but there is no time for "taking it slow." We are thrown into the world of intimate conversations about finances and future housing. I am elbow deep in boxes and closet cleaning so that we can stage his home for its sale. His trust in me gives me butterflies, and even when I stumble upon his old wedding video— "Oh, let's watch this," I immaturely tease—we laugh at the oddity of it all.

Every phone call from someone wanting to view the home triggers a flurry of cleaning, fluffing, stuffing, wiping, adjusting. We leave half-eaten meals and cash on restaurant tables so we can rush home to spruce the place up for showings.

"We're selling the home to live on a boat and tour the world," Kallan says to realtors.

"So, you're walking away from *everything?* All of this?" they ask. Kallan scoffs at that expected response. "They just don't get it," he explains to me later. I didn't get it either, so far. Much later, I'll come to understand that to some people, a constructed pile of wood and wires on a plot of land for a life of repetitive days *is* everything. Much, much later I'll come to understand that's entirely fine and just as beautiful. But not yet, so I just watch as Kallan walks the realtors from room to room pointing out details. Slowly, items disappear from his house. A fish sculpture that had previously rested on a shelf was sold to some neighbors. Art disappears. Dust-covered fake plants disappear. The desk with an almost-broken leg went to a nine-year-old with a newfound interest in drawing.

"Maybe he'll be an architect," his mother says with an anxious smile while pushing the desk into a car that's far too small to transport a desk. We squeeze it in anyway.

Everything plays out in front of me like theater. I see myself enter and exit scenes; I'm simultaneously a part of everything and floating in the air—above my own body—asking, "Who is this girl going along with it all?" I'm both shocked by and loving her.

***

"Sheena. Where are you?" I snap back from a daydream. My colleague is staring at me, tapping a pen on her desk. "Did you hear what I said?" I hadn't. I can't help but acknowledge the earth-splitting divide growing in my life. My "normal" life includes juggling my nine-to-five job, my part-time jobs, and my beach condominium. My life with Kallan includes selling a home, repairing a boat, and planning an exit from it all. With each passing day I'm more and more "in" with Kallan's mission. I come home to my beach condominium, and it feels un-lived in; I go to my job and I find myself uncommitted. I tell my friends that I'm just "busy," instead of the truth that I'm refurbishing a twenty-year-old boat to sail away from it all—which includes them.

It takes gargantuan effort to keep up the performance. I'm hocus-pocusing everyone around me but Kallan; to everyone else, I'm a hard worker who moves slowly into new relationships. To Kallan, I'm all in. I'm his partner on this life-changing adventure that will inevitably result in us setting sail. I think about Kallan walking real estate agent after real estate agent through the house; one of us is trying to visualize a new life; one is trying to say goodbye.

My phone rings. The house is under contract. Now we have thirty days to downsize from a 1,500-square-foot home to The Boat—our boat, our nine hundred square feet of *Seas Hope*.

"No, sorry. I didn't hear you," I say, refocusing on my colleague.

"Girl, you are out to sea," she says. She has no idea how accurate that is.

***

We schedule a massive yard sale to which nearly three hundred people show up in response to Kallan's online posting: "Everything must go! We're moving onto a boat to follow our dreams!" Kallan, Jimmy, and I are hauling boxes of—what feels like now—unnecessary surplus. *Who needs all of this anyway?* Some people show up for the severely discounted home goods and some show up "just to see who would be crazy enough to do such a thing," they tell us. Furniture, bedframes, mattresses, artwork, and kitchen utensils disappear. Our trio clinks our beers together as one by one, items walk their way out of our lives. What starts off at $5 in the morning will be priced at a nickel by late afternoon. This new life we are creating is happening one checked-off box at a time, and quite literally one box of sold goods at a time, and it is happening *fast*.

CHAPTER THREE

The Universe

After reading *The Alchemist*, I set it aside. *It's fiction,* I tell myself. The universe doesn't make dreams come true simply because you align your life choices and effort to your hopes (turns out that in this case, that *is* how it works, but I couldn't know that yet). I knew Kallan would love this book, but I wasn't ready to pass it on to him—reinforce his beliefs that the *universe* would help him into this boat? No, thanks. What he needed right now, I thought, was a dose of heartless reality, not dreamy-schemey fiction. Later, much later, I will reckon with this unfair projection. How unconsciously cruel of me to throw onto him my childhood anger of experiencing harsh takedowns or swift dismissals when it came to dreaming. But after our "I'm doing this with or without you" conversation, I hid the book so that he wouldn't accidentally stumble upon it. His reading this book—I selfishly feared—would only speed up an already overwhelming current of tireless dedication to this path. We were body-deep in boat projects—the kind that seem to unravel fast; one broken thing uncovering countless other broken things underneath. We needed help. Even without having read *The Alchemist,* Kallan was sure the universe would provide.

"Help will come along," he says confidently, his feet hanging over the side of a hammock he's strung up outside at my beach condominium. I roll my eyes and gulp down a swallow of fizzy water.

"Yeah, OK. Because someone wants to go sweat with you outside in nearly one-hundred-degree temperatures for eight hours a day scraping off toxic paint—*for free!*" I say, squishing into the hammock with him. Resting under his strong arms feels comforting. I am soothed by his scent, a mix of salted sweat, tobacco, and coconut shampoo. He kisses the top of my head.

"You'll see," he says. "Someone will appear. Someone will see it as an opportunity."

I am thankful for the grace Kallan gives me when it comes to my mountain of doubt, my exasperated huffs and vocalized assurances of failure. I wish I could believe with the ease he does. Or, at least, be able to silence my loudening disbelief. We kiss.

Enter Max. A twenty-four-year-old waiter who splits double shifts at two different seafood restaurants. With a knack for storytelling and a self-proclaimed talent for giving "excellent massages," Max entrances you with language and hilarity for hours before you realize that the crab-leg-and-waffles dish for two he slid across the table was finished off by just one, and that one was you. *Gulp.*

Max, Kallan tells me one day while showering off shards of fiberglass, has days off. Max, Kallan says, stepping out of the shower and wrapping a towel around his waist, believes in dreams. "He said he would love to help get the boat ready. For free." Kallan is smiling. I'm sitting on the bathroom floor watching this Adonis of a man—who is getting leaner and stronger every day from his work on the boat—smile at his goddamn *universal luck*. I shut down a thought in my head: The book said this would happen.

The day I meet Max, he comes bouncing across the street to introduce himself. Fresh off working my job and in my regularly scheduled numbed-out, frazzled state, I watch him and his bouncing glee approach.

"Hi, I'm Max!" he says, extending a hand. "I'm helping Kallan on the boat. You must be Sheena. I've heard a lot about you! I think I left my smokes." I walk up the stairs of the porch to the front door where Kallan comes bouncing out—literally. After working on a boat, men bounce, apparently.

"Yo, bro!" Kallan says, passing him his cigarettes. "Thanks for your work today, man. I really appreciate it." I stand there watching this scenario unfold, floored. "We ground out two whole hulls today!" Kallan says.

"Wow! That's incredible," I say, though I still barely know what that means.

"Alright, man, I've got to go to work now. I'll see you tomorrow—same time, same place!" Max says. Then he disappears with his smokes.

"So . . ." I say, following Kallan back inside "How much are you paying him?"

"Nothing," he says flatly, falling back on the couch to throw his arms behind his head.

"Nothing?" I throw my work bags down and scoot in next to him.

"*Nothing.* He wants to learn about boats." Inside, I know Kallan is bouncing—*yes, still bouncing, everyone is bouncing but me*—that stupid boat bounce; it's very similar to the "I told you so" bounce.

For four months, Max stands side by side with Kallan (and sometimes me) in Virginia's oppressive summer heat working on *Seas Hope* in exchange for occasional pizza, cold beer, or smokes. When I ask him why, he says without hesitation, "Man, it's important to help people with their dreams. You all are good people. I have time. And I'm learning things I didn't know how to do before. Win-win. *Seas Hope* is my opportunity to do something interesting right now." Free help had appeared into our lives, manifested from nothing—and Kallan was right: somebody saw this whole fiasco as an *opportunity*. His committed help sped up our project. Two extra hands, an extra mind, and a friend to laugh and vent with had arrived—for free. Universe: 1. Doubter Sheena: 0.

I often find myself wondering why one of us hasn't left this relationship. My doubter tendencies are conflicting . . . tiresome, even to me, so they have to be eating away at him. But for all of the differing feelings we've had about the boat, this plan of action, this squall of preparation, and this countdown to full-time boat living, we don't feel different about *us*, it seems. He still intrigues me. His driving passion seduces me. The way he devotes himself to speaking about "out there"—the open ocean and the freedom, the spiritedness that comes with it—there must be something out there that he's felt; something I can't come close to imagining. This intrigues me too. When we lie in bed cuddled up, the edges and angles of our bodies fit perfectly, effortlessly. This has to mean something. We exchange "I love you" on one of those nights, interwoven and kissing. We are doing hard life things together, and we're doing them while mostly laughing and kissing. This has to mean something. Even when we have the hard conversations, we both surface from them still not wanting to leave. This has to be that wild, free, savage love I've read about in books. He gives me a pass when it comes to my doubt, knowing there's no way anyone can know about "out there" until they've seen it, felt it, and let the magnificent immensity of it all make its way into your veins, changing the very way you move through life forever. So, we carry on. He lovingly—even through frustration—waits for me to "get on board" and I, lovingly full of doubt, stay dedicated to navigating my way there.

Having read *The Alchemist* and then seen with my own eyes Max manifest something from nothing, I would think I'd learn to trust the universe more—or at least put a significant dent in my fortress of doubt—but no. As the scenarios become more complex, so follows the doubt. It isn't long before Kallan put out another highly specific request of the universe.

Seas Hope, a Catamaran Catana 431, is French-made. All of its wiring is French, and the handwritten notes scribbled on tape to aid in fixing those wires . . . also in French. My strictly ballet-based knowledge of French limits me to general translations such as "open" and "closed." We are getting nowhere.

"I need a marine electrician . . . who speaks French . . . and will work for free," Kallan says one day, exasperated by a tangled mess of wires and French manuals. Right. Here we go again, except this time it's a terribly specific request for a French-speaking person with expert electrician-level knowledge of French marine wiring. I don't even roll my eyes or fight this time. The universe will show him his request is too much. I'm sure of it. We move on with our lives.

One day, my cellphone rings. "An old friend of mine is the head of a sailing school," Kallan starts. "They need help, and I was thinking I'd volunteer." He signs up to teach sailing to middle-school kids one day a week on the same night that I teach middle-school kids ballet.

We continue on with our lives, and one day my cellphone rings again.

"I invited my new friend over for dinner tonight—" Kallan says. I can tell by the glee in his voice what he's about to tell me: "—He's French." *No.* ". . . speaks French . . ." *No.* ". . . and he's a marine electrician."

NO.

Enter Marc, the French marine electrician Kallan met through volunteering at the sailing school. He moved here with his wife and son. She's in medical school, so he stays at home with their boy; he has some free time and he'd love to take a look, he says. Kallan invites him over to the boat, and we make him the best meal we can on a boat that's only partly in working order. While I stir pasta in boiling water, Marc helps Kallan sort through our floating French electrical headache. One by one, lights start to work, toilets start to flush, solar panels generate power. Marc's understanding of the French electrical mappings is bringing *Seas Hope* back to life. They solder weak electrical connections on panels and in the process resurrect lighting and pumps that haven't worked in ages—and that no one but Kallan believed would work again.

"Man, it feels good to be doing this kind of work again," Marc says, washing up his hands. "I've missed it." I plop pasta down in front of them once they're seated, and we eat under lights that are now working instead of by candlelight.

Witnessing Kallan manifest success irritates me. I am the one reeling with anxiety and fear, and the universe sends no one—*especially for free*—to help me. Does this work for Kallan and no one else? Why do I feel so unsupported and alone? *If the universe isn't broken, clearly, I am.* I recall an aggravating quote from Abraham Hicks I once saw printed on the side of a paper cup of coffee: "You can't watch out for bad things and allow good things at the same time. It is vibrationally not possible."

"OK, then, Universe," I say to myself aloud in the shower, long after guests are gone and dinner's dishes are cleaned. "Maybe you're waiting for me to own this thing; waiting for me to claim this path as my own; waiting for me to stop waiting for a savior from all of this doubt and believe a little bit." I step out of the shower and throw on a towel, leaving my hair dripping and stringy. Maybe waiting on a mind-blowing, singular breakthrough is not what changes my life here. Maybe a series of micro shifts is what I need. My fear of the unknown and my absolute resolution to not trust the universe will stand its sturdy ground unless I do something, try something, no matter how small.

I grab my laptop and log into Facebook, remembering a friend of mine had added me to a group called "Women Who Sail" a few months back. Today, I will make my first post and ask for help. *If the universe is going to step up and help ME, now is the time!*

> November 11, 2016:
>
> I met a sailor and we fell in love. He purchased a forty-three-foot catamaran and wants to travel the world six to twelve months from now! I have a lot of fear. I don't know the sailing world, that lifestyle, or even where to begin. Specifically: how to live on a boat; how to make money; what happens if we fall ill or get injured? My anxiety increases as his excitement increases. I want to learn this world—for him—and be open to experiencing it—for us—but I need some comfort, some guidance, a stronger knowledgebase to stand on than his excitement. Help? [Location: Norfolk, Virginia].

I post it and sit staring at the screen.

Where are you, universe?

My hair drips circular splashes onto my laptop.

Now is your time to help me, be present for me!

I feel my jaw tighten. I bob my leg nervously up and down.

This isn't going to work. The universe doesn't care who I am or what I need.

"Someone's typing" bubbles appear below my post. I lean in closer to the screen. Enter Jenn, Janice, and Suzie.

[We can teach you to sail.]

I read the comment aloud to myself. It hadn't even occurred to me to learn how to sail. Here I've been worrying about how to make money or find safety if injured, and it never occurred to me to just . . . learn how to sail to let a little wind into this story I'm living.

[5:00 p.m. Hampton Yacht Club.]

"UNIVERSE RESPONDS. GIRL TAKES NOTICE"

I finally pushed aside my stubbornness and dared *to ask.* These strangers heard my cry to the universe. They read between the lines to offer up what I didn't know I needed: a real, tangible ticket into this world—the chance to learn, to do on my own, to fall in love with sailing on my own terms, instead of just watching Kallan captain and enjoy. My fingers hover above the keys. I have a choice to make: Yes or no. Accept adventure and learn something outside of my non-belief in self, or decline and stand firm in my non-belief in, well, all of this.

I type, "Yes, please," hit Enter, then run and jump straight into the pillows on my bed, screaming in glee. When I remove the pillow from my face, I'm smiling.

One night after work, soon after the invitation, I speed to the Hampton Yacht Club. I find Jenn standing on the dock with a Lululemon bag and a smile. She knew I had no idea how to dress for this. Grateful, I change quickly in the bathroom. Then we run out to where the women are organizing for the race. *My first time learning how to sail, and it's under the pressure of a race. Sounds about right.*

Skippers are decided upon.

First mates are chosen.

Crew is designated. I note their terminology—words I've never heard before.

Jenn and I are placed on a twenty-three-foot Sonar with a skipper named Janice, a bubbly redhead who seems nice enough to trust my life with. *I guess the Universe has . . . got me?* We hop into our boats and my sailing lesson begins.

I watch how every line and sheet works: starboard, bow/stern, point of sail, helm, keel, heeling, tack, jibe, windward, leeward, lines, mainsail, jib. We round one of the markers and we're in second place. Now I'm excited! Jenn hands the line over to me, and now I'm tailing the jib and listening to the commands of the skipper.

"I refuse to lose to Annie!" Janice says. "If we lose, we have to make a sacrifice and the new girl goes!" I laugh because *that has to be a joke, right?* I look at Jenn who invited me to this whole thing and realize: I'm on a boat . . . with strangers . . . one of whom I met on the *Internet* . . . surrounded by water . . . .

Great, Sheena. Great. Go ahead, take the candy they're going to offer you next! Go look for their lost puppy with them! The universe led you straight to your drowning demise. Cool!

Janice stares at me with a straight face and says, "I'm serious." I nod and sit back, silently tailing the jib on command, eyeing the water, and calculating my chances for survival should Janice toss me overboard.

We come in second place that evening (Annie won), and it is decided that I may continue living. I receive a wine charm at the award ceremony, where I almost want to give a speech because wait . . . *did I have fun? Was that thrilling?* The wind from the bay tangles my hair as I thumb the wine charm in my pocket. *That was fun. This is doable. I am capable.*

Bitten by the sailing bug, I drive home to Kallan's arms. My clothes are off within seconds of entering the door. I push Kallan, smiling, onto the couch. I am becoming someone I wasn't before, and I like her better.

That night, I pull *The Alchemist* from underneath my folded T-shirts and hand it to Kallan. He reads the book in a day.

Nothing bad happens.

CHAPTER FOUR

A Weary Heart Opens

At West Marine, an employee (and our newest friend), Karen, is helping us solve convoluted problems by looking through photos on our iPhones.

"Can you zoom that in?" she asks, squinting her eyes for clues of a diagnosis. Kallan's hair is starting to grow long—a sure sign he's on his way out of corporate America. "Ah, yes. This piece is missing." She zooms in further. "This piece is rusted." She tilts the phone to the side. "Do you know where this wire leads?"

She fills our arms with screws, piping, tanks, chain, and backups of everything should something fall overboard or into an irretrievable crevice of the boat's hull. A typical West Marine receipt exceeds $1,000, and we're at this store multiple times a week. Screws, piping, tanks, chain, and backups chomp away at that home-sale profit.

We become masters at boat yoga, standing in precarious positions to squeeze through tiny nooks, slithering through cutouts to trace wires, all while balancing tools in both hands. "Cahn yoo reech that?" we ask through lips pursed together to hold whatever screw, piece of tape, brush, or sandpaper we'll be using.

With all the construction, financial gyrations, and relationship tension *Seas Hope* is putting us through, we are learning how to pull together through chaos, clutter, and overwhelm. Each day we tackle what we can. Each night we plot, plan, and cuddle. Kallan sketches out maps, ideas, blueprints. He scribbles on napkins to lay out the next day's plans. When something tries to pull us apart, like exhaustion, frustration, differing opinions, or some unexpected, exceedingly expensive problem, we hunker in closer. We are what we have. We are learning to care for each other while learning to care for the boat, which is finally starting to feel a little more like *our boat.*

My heart is learning to love in new ways.

- Loving without needing approval or permission from others.
- Loving myself as competent.
- Loving without needing to know the outcome.
- Loving with a hopeful, building spirit.
- Loving in a way that stays in constant contact with our inherent goodness.
- Loving that provides support even though I can't see the end vision.

I ask myself questions: *What happens if I just keep showing up? For him? For me? For the boat? What if I choose to believe first instead of doubt first? What could happen outside of what I think will happen? What happens if I wait and see what the universe wants to show me?* We always find our place together—again and again—by gifting ourselves some kindnesses: We express excitement when we see each other in the morning, and after periods of time away. "Just like puppies," Kallan would say. We vocalize our joy whenever one of us calls the other—even if it's to deliver stressful news. We treat ourselves to meals together, even if dinner means grabbing a pizza and eating it on the bow of our boat (which, during some phases of its renovation, sits on land). We delight in small treasures: lighting candles for romance; splitting the tiramisu; taking breaks to sing, dance, or walk by the water's edge. We hold hands. We laugh at our jokes. We cry when we're frustrated. Our love is expanding who we are, and preparing us for what's to come.

***

It's June 25, 2017, a sunny day at my Virginia Beach oceanfront condo—which we have packed up. After the sale of Kallan's house, we split our time between my condo and the boat until she was repaired enough to be livable. Now, she's livable. Now, it's *Go* Time. No more land-living options. It's boat or bust.

Trash bags of clothes: donated.

Fancy kitchen items: sold.

Non-boat-friendly furniture: sold.

Beach condo: rented out. I hand over the keys. I am sure my new tenants can see my hands shaking. Each night leading up to this moment, I've dreamed of rogue waves. I saw a picture of one in a sailing book. Underneath an image of a curling, foaming-at-the-mouth wave that appears to have sought out the small vessel was a definition: unusually large, unpredictable, and suddenly appearing surface waves that can be extremely dangerous to ships, even to large ones. In my dream, the wall of water is impossible to survive. You can't swim under it—the rolling power is too strong underneath. You can't go over it because no ship can mount a vertical wall of moving water or endure the imminent fall awaiting them on the other side of the wave. You can only hope it destroys you faster than your brain can register the pain. Passing my keys over to my tenants feels unusually large, unpredictable, and sudden of me; a powerful bang side-swiping my cookie-cutter life.

"Be kind to my condo," I plead with a shaky voice.

"We'll show it a lot of love," says, my tenant, Chloe, closing her fingers around the key. Handing over my worldly possessions feels like pulling off one octopus tentacle at a time as if these items were somehow stuck to me, as if it's my life's duty to keep and maintain them. Once I work through the psychological warfare of pulling each one off, a sense of freedom rushes in, but so do the comments from people who don't understand:

"This is why we get jobs," people would tell me. "To buy things. To keep things."

"These are great clothes! I can't believe you're giving this all away."

"What a waste of your precious time, energy, and money," I was told when I left behind my $1,500 bedroom suite for my tenants to use for free.

These comments send a very clear message: work hard to get things and then work harder to keep them forever. When your house is too full, get a bigger house, not a smaller life. I *worked* to buy these items. Then worked to buy more items to organize and display said items. I started to agree; it does feel wasteful! But not because I'm giving them up—it feels wasteful to live only to consume *items*.

After I hand over the keys to my condominium, ninety-eight percent of my worldly possessions are gone, and the only place I can call "home" is a boat. Jimmy helps us toss what belongings we've kept onto the boat before he heads to his new apartment, a place he had to find after his roommates gave up land living. I unpack the bag of clothes I kept—bathing suits, T-shirts, shorts, some pants, sundresses—and I recall something a man said to me one evening at the marina: "You can't live with one foot on the boat and one foot on the dock. The space between the boat and the dock grows wider. Indecision creates a lot of hardship." Well, I'm both feet in now. I'm saying *yes* to Kallan's personal legend. We are doing this thing. We are trusting the universe. We are choosing each other. Home address: floating on the Chesapeake Bay. And maybe, just maybe, it could lead to a personal legend for me, too—which I haven't believed until now.

***

In many ways, life is easier after jumping in with both feet. Whole conversations and stressors we previously had, disappear. We are no longer maintaining two homes, no longer splitting our time or energy. Kallan paid off the boat with his home sale, leaving him with zero mortgages, and my mortgage is covered by my renters. We pay rent to the marina for our boat slip. Dockage includes 30-amp or twin 50-amp power, use of a communal bathroom and pool, mail delivery at the marina office, and waste pickup. It costs $12 per foot per month, and since we're forty-three-feet, that puts us at $516 per month—pennies compared to the thousands of dollars we just offboarded in mortgages. Relief from financial pressure opens up a lot of potential opportunity—like not needing to work so many jobs—but we decide to stay the path and save as much money as we can. I get to learning a new way of living using Maslow's hierarchy of needs as my guide.

First need, shelter: I move around my new space, my eyes taking in every crack, crevice, and cushion. I open all of the windows to let in sunlight and fresh air. There are two sleeping quarters, one in each hull, with the galley in between the two hulls. The bed cushions rest on wooden slats creating hidden storage underneath. I pull them out, scrub them down then set them in the sun to air out. There are two bathrooms. I scrub down the showers with environmentally friendly pure Castile soap, knowing anything I use will go down the drain and into the bay we're floating on. I become familiar with the lines that run underneath the floors moving all human waste to a holding tank, which we're responsible for emptying at fuel docks that have a waste pump-out option. I put away dishes, pots, and pans in cabinets that lock so they don't come crashing out with the waves. I sweep. I dust. We replaced the stereo before we moved in, so now we can play music throughout the boat, and I'm glad. We catch each other dancing and singing as we settle into our new nest. I put my clothes away, piece by piece. Kallan has one closet and I have one. We hang our clothes on plastic hangers because metal hangers would rust within three months due to saltwater and air exposure. In the third closet we house extra linens, towels, and compostable toilet paper. We have five drawers to split. There is a pantry for dry goods, and a refrigerator that opens from the top—you have to dive in to get to the food. If I'm trying to reach something at the very bottom, I lean all the way in, head down, feet counterbalancing in the air. The galley (kitchen) has a stove with two burners fueled by gas coming from one of two propane tanks—another necessity that must be replenished when it runs out, just like drinking water and boat oil. There is an office with a desk lamp. Windows are everywhere; they open and close with locks to seal them, though water occasionally seeps in. In my head, I start to understand the functionality of the vessel in terms of "what comes in and what goes out."

What comes in:

1. Electricity, which we can get either by connecting to shore power or from the sun by using solar panels to charge our six batteries.
2. Fresh, potable water for drinking and showering; we access fresh water either from a marina via a hose, or by collecting rainwater and filling the freshwater tanks.
3. Salt water, which comes in via foot pump for washing dishes. This saves the fresh water supply.
4. Diesel fuel and boat oil for the engine. Propane gas for cooking.
5. Provisions (food) and supplies (medical; hygiene; boat cleaning).

What goes out:

1. Certain drains go straight out into the water, so a heightened awareness is required when putting anything down those drains.

2. Human waste, via the holding tank.
3. Biodegradable waste, municipal solid waste (plastic, packaging), and recycling—which we off-board and dispose of properly.

I start to see her—our boat—as a living, breathing being with her own personality and spirit. She takes; she gives; and every choice we make matters, since we are her caretakers. She's family now.

Outside, there is a built-in bench with hatches that open to store life vests, boat oil, and tools, and a wooden table for serving outdoor meals and laying out charts. Since this is a catamaran, there are two helms—or wheels—for steering: one on the port (left) side and one on the starboard (right) side. The cushions are cracked open due to sun and saltwater exposure, but they work just fine. I walk down the side of the vessel to the trampoline, an area of high-strength material under high tension stretched between the two hulls of the vessel. The material is woven together in strips, which makes for an open "deck" of sorts that water can splash through. It's a romantic stargazing place, but in high seas, it'll splash a sailor right off the vessel. I sit down and take it all in.

Maslow's second need, safety and security:

We have fire and carbon monoxide alarms as well as fire extinguishers. We made sure that all of the electrical wiring was properly grounded because we heard stories of people being electrocuted while climbing down their metal ladders into the water. We have first aid kits within easy reach, and we've purchased an emergency position-indicating radio beacon (EPIRB) to use while sailing. EPIRBs are emergency locators for commercial and recreational boats. Portable, battery-powered, and user-friendly. If people out at sea find themselves in distress—a medical emergency or a sinking ship, for example—they can press a button and it will transmit a distress radio signal to search-and-rescue teams who can render aid. I take a boating safety course and check out books at the library on the mechanics of large bodies of water, weather, and sailing rules. I only make it halfway through a book on the nature of the ocean, but the gist of it seems to be that pools of water, from small puddles of rain to our earth's oceans, behave similarly when exposed to the forces of energy from the sun, movement of land masses, wind, and gravity. So, the book suggests, to learn about the ocean, I should start with poking around in a puddle. I return the book and become increasingly aware of puddles.

Maslow's third need, love and belonging:

Kallan is re-energized by us moving onboard. Any exhaustion he felt by the year's worth of repairs and his home sale—*poof!*—gone. With this revitalization he showers love onto me, and I soak it all up. A love that feels exciting has a way of making every cell in my body buzz with glee.

But belonging on *Seas Hope* feels more complex to me. Since it isn't technically *my* boat, and I'm still learning the ways of the liveaboard lifestyle, I find myself hesitating to claim space. Kallan notices and responds with a beautiful act of love.

Long before meeting Kallan, I had purchased a driftwood turtle. For some reason I wanted to keep it, even though I knew it was silly—art hanging on the walls of a perpetually moving vessel? Kallan had suggested I give it away, but when I protested, he didn't. Our first day living onboard, he notices my private struggle with belonging. I sit, not knowing what to touch or not touch; not knowing if it's okay to decorate something or not. Without hesitation, he digs out the driftwood turtle from a box, grabs a hammer and nail and before I can say, "No, don't!" he thrusts the nail into the treasured walls of his *vintage* catamaran vessel—something no sane, vintage boat-owner would do. Then he turns to me and says, "This is your home too."

The fourth Maslow need, esteem:

My confidence is growing. I learn the inner workings of the vessel. I spend time with other liveaboard families who pass along tips and tricks. I continue my sailing lessons. I grow from my mistakes—like when I tried to control the line of the jib but the wind yanked it from my hand, leaving behind a bleeding, raw rope burn. Takeaway: the wind will always be stronger than I am, but I can build up my instincts and knowledge. The more I get to know these forces of nature, the better I can anticipate and know how to work with their presence.

And, finally, the fifth need, self-actualization:

I hope this will come. There is still a scary cloud looming over me: sailing away from it all. I gift myself grace in this category and continue to wade through the unknown while holding down my jobs.

A few weeks into boat living and the dreamy nature of it gives way to reality. On workdays, I get up every morning and pull on the one pair of pants and a button-up blouse I kept for work. I grab an apple from the hanging fruit basket. I'd prefer a banana, but bananas on boats are bad luck—a superstition originating from the 1700s, when trade ships sailing from the Caribbean disappeared and the only remnants left of the vessels was their floating cargo: a lot of bananas. I grab my bag with my laptop and then, very cautiously, jump from the deck of the boat to the marina dock hoping my laptop doesn't accidentally tip from my bag and land in the water. A big exhale. I make it. I drive from the boat into work each day, but nobody I work with knows about the boat yet. They still think I'm regular Sheena doing regular Sheena life driving from my regular Sheena condo.

After work, one day, I find that the wind is pushing—and holding—the boat to the ends of the lines, tethering her to the dock. I can't possibly jump that far to get back onto the boat. I set my bag down and walk over to one of the lines and pull, pull, pull. I am grunting, fighting the wind, my feet are sliding out from underneath me trying to pull this massive boat toward me. She moves a little, but by the time I drop the line and grab my bag, the wind moves her right back to where she was. *Sigh.* I think to myself, *None of my friends have to pull their homes toward them just to get inside.*

"Need some help?" A boat neighbor says. His arms are full of grocery bags, but he sets them down and comes over. "You get ready to board." He picks up the lines and prepares his hands. "1 . . . 2 . . ." He's preparing to squat. "3 . . ." I jump and he lets go of the line and the wind pushes her, pulling the line taut.

"Thank you! I would've had to sit outside for a long time."

"Boat people do life together." He picks up his groceries. "Welcome to the neighborhood."

Onboard life means:

1. Having to move heavy grocery bags from the dock to the boat.
2. Always jumping on and off.
3. Balancing while on the boat, especially during agitated weather.

4. Twisting to catch an object that a wave or wake sends sliding toward the floor.
5. Ducking your head so you don't knock yourself out when entering or exiting the cabin.
6. Holding on to something while trying to use the bathroom.
7. Adjusting the lines holding your boat to the dock with every change in tide, wind, or weather.
8. Checking levels of electricity, fresh water, oil, and waste every day.
9. Everything feeling damp when it rains.

A few events like that under my belt and I find myself physically drained. I think of the looming cloud: Kallan wants to sail soon. How will I possibly do this out in the middle of the ocean without a dock or solid ground to escape to? But sailing is clearly still his plan, and it's coming closer and closer with every completed repair.

I walk nervously down the dock one day to talk to a woman who lives alone on her boat. She stands before me, oil-covered, cranking down on a stubborn bolt, a coffee cup full of oil beside her.

"Sheena, what are you so damned afraid of? Seriously?" she asks, throwing down a wrench and placing her hand on her hip while wiping sweat from her brow. She's from my parents' generation. She doesn't have time for my millennial angst. She grabs the coffee cup and swallows the contents. *So . . . not oil then?*

"Of *dying*, obviously!" I answer.

"You aren't afraid of dying, Sheena. That's a bullshit answer and a waste of my boat's time." She sits her tired body down and pours some whiskey in the coffee/boat oil cup. "When you throw a lightbulb into the ocean, what happens?" In my head I see a wave smash the delicate lightbulb into a thousand pieces, sending it shattered into the sea to one day become sand.

"It floats." She answers for me, an answer I couldn't even fathom. "The ocean doesn't crush it, explode it, spit it back out, and say, 'I told you not to come in here! I told you that you would fail!' The ocean cradles it and carries it to a new destination."

"Then . . . I'm scared of having no money, since we'll have no jobs."

"You'll make money out there, but also you don't die the second your bank account reaches zero. Trust me." And she disappears below deck. What am I really afraid of?

I walk around the marina hearing the clinks and clanks of boats rocking with the wind looking for some mental clarity. I've wrestled with lack of self-esteem and hulking forms of doubt—internal and external—to be standing here today, but now it's time to wrestle with fear.

I'd kept Kallan's sailing dream secret from my family, friends and work colleagues for as long as I could, mostly because I figured at any point something could derail our speeding train. What good could come from worrying everyone else with his moon-shot dream? But after the yard sale, Kallan's home sale, and now with my condo rented out, it's no longer a moon shot. It's happening. When a parent calls to say, "I'd love to come for a visit," and they're expecting my beach condominium, I have to explain that the guest room is now, well, floating.

I hadn't wanted to tell anyone—correction: I am *still* afraid to tell everyone, even now as I walk around in circles at our marina. Maybe the answer to her question, "What are you so damned afraid of?" is actually "Giving myself permission to disappoint the expectations my family projects onto me that don't match my heart's desire." *Ouch.*

Leaving it all to go sailing is on brand for Kallan. His family wasn't surprised in the slightest when he called to say: "I bought a boat!" Kallan's father owns a sailboat that floats in a slip a few docks over from ours. My family? I come from a line of play-it-safe preachers, teachers, administrators, railroad workers, tobacco farmers and production engineers. The only seafaring adventurers I know about were the hungry souls who crossed the sea from Ireland (paternal side) and Hungary (maternal side) with their eyes set on the American dream. They arrived ready to work and since then, we've been hunkered down, quietly working hard, relinquishing personal ambitions and dreams to care for our families. If dreams weren't banished or forced to live in exile, they were forced into place by "sure, you can do that—as a hobby."

As a kid, I had a lot of rage around that limit. I just couldn't wrap my head around it. "You pay taxes and then you die," I'd often hear. Once I became a tax-paying adult, I started to understand more: living, much more raising children, isn't easy in a culture that requires over-productivity to feel valued. Add in normalizing the suppression of feelings in a system where obedience and compliance are demanded with—icing on the cake—a prevailing sense of scarcity when it comes to money, time, love and energy, and we're left with a lot of exhausted Americans with little time to dream. My parents worked hard to provide for my brother and me, and that took all of their money, time and energy. I have few to no memories of watching my parents do what they wanted to do simply because they wanted to do it. Adult spontaneity was in low supply. But I was very aware of how locked in we all were when it came to what they had to do. I also knew that if they didn't do what was required, there was some form of punitive result awaiting them which would eventually hurt me too. So, I grew up unconsciously equating feelings of freedom and joy with punishment. They were simply telling me what the world had already screamed at them: "Always think of what other people want you to do. If you want something for yourself, you can do that—*only as a hobby*." This approach, applied over generations, resulted in ever-growing security for my family line. By the time it got to my brother and me, we didn't worry about affording a comfortable home, getting food on our tables, paying electricity bills—we even got ballet and soccer lessons!

So, I get it. I do. Safety and security yield results. Results I benefited from. It's why I've put off telling them because it's hard to ask them to understand something I still don't have the words for myself: This isn't working for me. There has to be something else other than . . . *lifting my hands up at the world they helped me create* *this*. Feelings of guilt roll over me when I even think about telling them. But I gave away my condo, my backup plan, my "in case of emergency, break glass" safety option. I did that because I knew that if I decided not to sail, and stayed in my condo, that choice wouldn't be a win. I'd be keeping the sameness that had been slowly killing me. I'd lose the adventure *and* Kallan, and then have to forever tell the tale of what *almost* happened for me—who I *could have been*, what I *could have done*.

I have to tell them.

I open the curtains on what we've been up to. It's time.

"Kallan bought a boat."

"Good for him."

"And he sold his house."

"That's nice."

G*ulp. Just say it.*

"And I rented out my condo. And we're living together on the boat. And we're leaving. To go sailing."

It's less like dipping my toe into a cold pool of water and more like a cannonball: all in. Splash guaranteed. Gawkers assured. Everything is public. My family, my friends, my colleagues, now everyone knows we live full-time on *Seas Hope* and we're planning to leave for full-time sailing. Departure date: Unknown. Destination: Unknown. Return date: None.

Earthquakes of questions.

"What?"

"Why?"

"When?"

"How?"

"How could you?"

A tsunami of "because-we-love-you" responses.

"We're concerned."

"This isn't you."

"What if something bad happens?"

Tornados of judgments.

"Crazy."

"Insane."

"Brainwashed."

"Manipulated."

"So sad."

"What a waste of talent."

All the confidence I had gathered up slips back into deep shame. I haven't found the courage yet to slough off feelings of obligation to family, friends, and work so when they hurt, I hurt. *I feel sick.*

My going away throws them into a storyline they never asked for: to be left ashore; to worry if I've been plunged toward a watery death; to endure holidays, family gatherings, and *living* without me—their daughter, friend, colleague. When I stumble through attempts to answer their teary-filled question of "why?" I seem only to incite the frustration and anger that lives under the reality of "Well, obviously we all want *more!* But we don't get it!"

I sit and take it—their words, their fear. It's all valid. I remind myself that I want intrigue, challenge, boldness, bravery and this is my opportunity. When the boiling emotions cool down to a quieted simmer, they still need more answers.

"And how *exactly* do you plan to pull this off?"

They want a neat, easily digestible package of "trip" details:

How long will you be gone? What about money? Is it safe? What about everything you've built here?

I shrug. I don't have those answers yet, and I struggle to find words to convey that what we're doing is a lifestyle shift, not a vacation.

They shake their heads. "Life doesn't work like that, Sheena. What if everyone just up and disappeared to enjoy their dreams? The economy would collapse. This all seems very selfish."

When I finally make it back to the boat, I am raw, wide-open, vulnerable. These people I love, armed with words, logic, and familiarity with me, know that what they say to me matters, know their opinions carry weight. It isn't going to be easy to dismiss them. I crawl into bed with their voices still in my head: "It seems very unlike you to leave everything you've worked so hard for. The cost seems very high."

What is the cost if I listen to everyone else? Why are they making this the story of my whole life instead of a story of the next unknown number of months? Why is my want for adventure so threatening to them? What about this lifestyle offends others to such an aggressive degree? I feel the shift in my own reasoning—mine, not Kallan's, mine alone—and it feels good.

Dear World: I'm going.

***

Seas Hope is looking better, stronger, and more confident. She's filling with life—as am I—with the presence of our daily living. The barnacles are scraped off. The twin hulls are re-fiberglassed, sanded, and painted. The plumbing is working better. Yes, the lights flicker, but they mostly provide light. My onlooker friends keep shaking their heads. One even not-so-jokingly calls me homeless.

When I was in elementary school, a NASA representative showed us a map of the stars and our solar system—speckles and dots on poster board. She spoke with passion.

"About 13.8 billion years ago, our universe was just a ball of hot plasma. Can you imagine?" She passed a ball of orange Play-

Doh around for us to squeeze through our tiny fingers. "And then, there was sound. Sound waves, like ripples in a rain puddle, moved their way through the hot ball of plasma, and left an imprint." She grabbed the orange Play-Doh and left her thumb print right in the middle. "And here we are. Life is movement, and movement requires friction, and friction means sound. Any questions?"

She folded her map of the galaxy and headed out, but I remembered: *Life is movement, and movement requires friction, and friction means sound.*

The opinions, a heavy wall of sound, pour in and leave their imprint. *Life takes movement, and movement takes sound.* All these opinions remind me of a bigger picture—one even bigger than the ball of plasma that became the universe: *Sheena, you're alive. You're alive. You're alive.*

On August 12, 2017, less than twenty days after moving aboard *Seas Hope* full-time, we pick up a newspaper thrown on the dock beside our boat. An article—sizable, bright, and colorful—describes Kallan's dream. "Seizing Life by the Sails," the headline reads—a *real* headline, not one I've made up in my own mind. The article includes my name and image and how I've served as first mate in life and in repairs. The newspaper posts the article on their Facebook page. Comments pour in:

"Stupid."

"These people are going to get out there and die." *Life is movement, and movement requires friction, and friction means sound.*

"How is this news?"

"Must be nice to be rich." I sit at a coffee shop scrolling through the comments. These people don't know us or the extent of how beat-up our boat is or how little our budget is. I close my laptop.

Less than one week later, the CEO at my full-time job fires me during my lunch break, seconds after I unwrap my sandwich and take my first bite. She saw the article, she says. I swallow the bite. And if I plan to sail off into the sunset, my loyalties certainly aren't with my job.

"So, you can leave now," she says, dropping a box on my desk. I pack up my office trinkets and drive home to *Seas Hope.* I throw the box in the trash at the marina, and after a quick change, toss out my last pair of work pants, too.

Kallan, surprised to see me home early, scoots in next to me at the helm where I'm tossing sunflower seeds to seagulls.

"They fired me."

"We'll be just fine." He hugs me in close. "Now there's nothing holding us back from leaving."

I wake up the next day as a freshly fired, full-time boat dweller. As I push down my French press and make morning coffee, Kallan kisses my cheek. I catch myself smiling.

CHAPTER FIVE

Time to Go

With my work schedule cleared (*thank you, Universe*), it is time to leave. I have no remaining excuses to hold off Kallan's readiness to go. His home: sold. His job: finished. My condo: rented. My job: gone.

I have accepted that my "readiness" is not likely to come around, ever—at least not in the way Kallan's readiness looks. He's excited, confident, and this whole journey is family-endorsed. I'm apprehensive, suspicious, and still helping my family wrap their hearts and heads around it all. The weather window to leave opens. Big moments in life come on their own time-and-readiness table, and this moment was ready. My work: stay open and trust.

The night before we set sail, we buy $500 of groceries—mostly dry goods—and as we're securing the groceries for sea travel, I get a text from my friend: "I know you're leaving and you don't know when you'll be back, so I want you to meet my new boyfriend. It's important. He's important."

I feel a twinge of sadness. I hadn't thought my leaving would matter too much to others. But on Thanksgiving, as I parked my car at my mother's for who knows how long, I could feel her sadness, her fear. Her baby was about to go do something unheard of in our family's history. I could die—just as I could die driving a car down the street—but for some reason, this unknown feels scarier. I had a community of liveaboard families and sailors to help me work through that, but she didn't. I hadn't realized that my leaving, my choice of risk tasking, was also forcing her to reckon with the potential consequences as well. She cried when I drove away, and now I'm feeling that sadness again.

My friend, Christian, brings the new boyfriend, Geoff, who helps us unpack and secure heavy bags of rice, beans, and canned vegetables. We chat as we secure the pantry so that nothing flies out while we're offshore, then I hug my friend goodbye. They eventually go on to have their first child while I'm out sailing, and then marry and have another daughter. She was right. Meeting him that night was important.

We spend the day going over final preparations. We check off: food, clothes, shoes, toiletries, back-up boat parts, first aid kit, GPS tracking systems, chargers. There is no fancy dock party to see us off. We had our "we promise we'll be back some day" moments with our families at Thanksgiving, leaving them the keys to our parked cars. Now it's just us: Kallan, me, and *Seas Hope*. We lock down everything we can, and then the flurry of activity . . . stops. The only sound is the water lapping against the hulls, and the wind that we'll soon catch to carry us away. We look at each other and slowly exhale in unison.

"Ready?" he asks.

The dock lines weave around a cleat in a figure eight; an infinity symbol reminding me there is no plan, no return date, no plotted course. Unweave the figure eight and we float away into the infinite. I stand there staring at the line that keeps me attached to everything: land, my old life, my home state, my friends and family, my old approaches, and my patterns of understanding. For the last year-and-a-half I fretted over this very moment. I cried and chewed my fingernails nearly off over *this* moment. Someone has to unweave this line, set free this boat and these people for this dream to work. I know—and Kallan knows—that someone needs to be me. He looks at me and smiles, motioning toward the cleat.

I grab the line. Memories flood back. The anxiety. The tears. The fights.

I unweave the first wrap. I had fought Kallan fiercely through this process, because it was the only way I knew how to express, *I am scared. I am overwhelmed. Help me?* We nearly lost our relationship countless times. We made it through the storm, barely, just to make it to this starting line.

I pause before unwrapping the final turn around the cleat. Kallan is smiling. I untie the line that keeps *Seas Hope* tethered to the dock (and everything I know).

We made it. We did it. Freed, *Seas Hope* floats away.

It will be a very long time before we round this corner again, and when we do—*if* we do—I imagine we'll be very different people. I look over at Kallan, the wind blows through his now-long hair. He's waited for this. My friend who lives in a condominium on the edge of the water snaps a photo of us and posts it online declaring our exit from this world and into another, captioning it: "Fair winds and following seas! They're off!"

We are internet official—*gone.* Kallan lets out a primal cry of glee, head tilted back—a wolf howling at the moon. He's here for his personal legend. I squint to protect my eyes from the crisp November wind. I push the zipper of my jacket toward my throat and pull down on my winter cap. The sun is going down and we'll soon be met with the Atlantic Ocean—and darkness. I've never been out in the open ocean, "offshore," as seamen call it. I grab my journal and push the pen into the paper with so much adrenaline that when I returned to it later, I could feel the letters embossed into the page:

LIVE FULLY
LIVE IMMEDIATELY!
LIVE UNRESERVEDLY
LET GO ECSTATICALLY!
SHEENA, YOU'RE ALIVE!

PART TWO

The brave, they do not live forever, but the cautious, they do not live at all.

—Richard Branson

CHAPTER SIX

FINDING MY SEA LEGS

As a child, I stood on the shore for hours thinking, *I can swim to China.* I always dreamed about going "out there." If someone—even today—snapped a photo of my heart, the center of it would reveal a little girl in a purple swimsuit standing on the edge of the Atlantic Ocean, gazing out toward the horizon, wishing to know "out there." Now I'm on my way.

When I was ten, I asked my dad to take me offshore fishing.

"You're too young," he said. In that moment my spirit deflated the same way it did when an amusement park employee told me I was "too short" to ride the rollercoaster. What was the age, then, that the ocean's core became open to me? Like my roller-coaster-worthy height, I was determined to grow tall enough for *out there.*

While waiting to grow, I would watch when the offshore vessels returned with drunken, jovial men throwing their slippery, scaly, smelly haul—*thunk!*—onto the dock. Where did these fishermen go to find such heavy fish, rounded with meat? These fish looked different than the small carp and trout I pulled from smaller bodies of water—where people my age and height were permitted to fish. These were "real fish," "grown-up" fish. *Where was this magical, life-giving, body-filling place?* The only direction I ever received was cracked, oil-and-blood-covered fingers vaguely pointing, "offshore."

Splash. The bite of a cold wave hits me. I hug my arms around myself. *What if the universe hates me and conjures up deadly waves and speedy winds to spit me out? What if I become nauseated when I'm unable to see land?* Whatever happens, happens; I've thrown up before from nights of drinking away my land sorrows. We round the corner where the Chesapeake Bay turns into the Atlantic Ocean.

"We're in the ocean," Kallan reports, still beaming. I look around. Nothing changes. We adjust the sails and head farther out. The land shrinks to a small sliver and then becomes invisible. *Offshore* hasn't reached out to strike me dead, yet. *Why had I imagined you'd hate me so?*

"Something is off with our steering," I hear Kallan say. He looks at me, worried. "Should we turn around?" I imagine the headline:

"BRAVE COUPLE MAKES IT ALL OF ONE NAUTICAL MILE AND TURNS AROUND"

We wait for a second, attempting to gauge each other's panic level but we know our answer. No. We won't turn around. A new rule now applies to our new life: We make do with what we have when and where we have it. We'll keep going and fix whatever needs fixing along the way, even if that means frantically scooping water from our boat to delay sinking.

"COUPLE FOLLOWS THROUGH"

I am puffed up, wearing long johns, sweater, sweatshirt, scarf, hat, gloves, multiple pairs of socks, foul-weather gear, a jacket, and boots. In a few hours, the month will change to December. We are sailing on the open ocean where the wind doesn't understand my human need for a pause so that my skin can warm or rest from being blistered by cold. It just keeps blowing. Wanting to be a turtle, I pull my scarf over my mouth to keep my lips warm. I dream of golden blueberry muffins—not the gas station kind—being pulled from an oven, hot towels fresh from the dryer, fuzzy socks under comfy blankets. . . .

Lights appear in the distance. "It's another boat," I say, pointing to the light. "I wonder if they have a woman onboard!" *Someone else is out here? Other people do this? Maybe I'm not as crazy as people have accused me of being.* New to "boat life" or "cruising life," as full-time, boat-dwelling travelers call it, I am eager to learn from people—especially from women—more experienced than me. I grab the radio and hold down the button on the microphone.

"Sailing vessel rounding Cape Henry Lighthouse, entering the Atlantic Ocean. This is *Seas Hope.* Over." *Please answer, please answer, please answer.*

A man's voice answers.

"*Seas Hope*, this is *Southern Cross*; go ahead."

"Do you . . . uh . . . by chance, maybe . . . have a woman onboard?" I realize how crazy a question this is at 7:00 p.m.—or at any time on any night, for that matter. "Over."

"My wife is here. Over."

"Great! May I talk to her?" One thing I have learned from the online chat in Women Who Sail is that their approach to teaching sailing, connecting while sailing, and sometimes even their roles in sailing are different. I appreciated the feedback and support I've received virtually, and now I'm unafraid to ask for it. Dierdre ("D") Wogaman, I find out, is also a member in that online group of seafaring women, so she didn't find my radio request for connection odd at all.

She comes on the radio and as we float on the ocean, together but apart, I talk for hours to a stranger I can't see. I see the lights from their boat bobbing up and down on the same waves we ride. And her voice sends waves of comfort through me. We talk throughout the night about our lives, our *boat* lives, our plans, her experiences, her advice. "This is my first night out on the open ocean. Over." The radio goes silent for a moment.

"I'm honored to share it with you. Over."

We talk through dinner and a hot chocolate, then we put some miles between our boats to avoid a collision during sleeping shifts and night watches. We travel together with these new friends on the open ocean for two days. I never get to formally meet her. The closest we get is when we both pull into The Bright, Cape Lookout, North Carolina for rest and repairs. Kallan and I wake up with intentions to continue south, and they wake up to head their own way. Our boats pass with only five feet of water between us. She and I stand on the bows of our boats and wave to each other.

She cups her hands around her lips and yells, "You'll love this!" A complete stranger talked me lovingly and patiently through my first night at sea. I heard her love for the sea and felt her serenity through the radio. She told me all that was possible, including living in and enjoying this sailing life. Her best gift to me: She didn't tell me I couldn't.

* * *

I rub my eyes and stretch my arms. Morning. The sun is on the verge of rising. The world around me is still pitch black, but if I look closely enough, I can see a patch of sky giving in to navy, deep purple, lavender, and then pink. The giving in of night to day and day to night fills me with ease. *Why does anyone struggle for control?* I am bobbing, cradled, and enthralled.

The morning ribbon of colors means it's time to relieve Kallan of his watch. The person coming off watch always prepares coffee for the person starting watch, so I grab a cup and pour myself some of the hot, steaming coffee. I tighten my scarf and head out into the cold.

Monday. I would usually be waking up for work right now. I would pour my coffee to-go instead of enjoying it outside under a full sky. I would sit agitated while dodging traffic. This Monday morning, I've witnessed an alluring display of light tenderly passing on the baton. I kiss my partner good morning and we sit in the frigid chill watching the sun crawl into his spot in the sky—it's time for his watch, too. Cool air fills my lungs, tickles my cheeks. I wrap my fingers around my coffee cup for warmth and hold it up. Steam dances on my lips. Kallan smiles.

Usually, coming off a night watch is exhausting. Night watches require that someone remain awake to mind the boat's navigation and observe changes in the weather and winds. That person is responsible for guarding against collisions with other vessels or deadly, floating containers, full of stuff we buy from merchandise retailers, that has fallen off ships. I found out about night watches on our first night out, when my eyes were sleepy. Kallan caught me thinking we were both about to go to sleep. At the same time. Together.

"Are you ready for bed?" I asked. "I am."

"Do you want me to take the first shift?"

"Shift?"

"Yeah. Someone has to stay awake at all times when the boat is moving." The only way all people on board can sleep at the same time is if the vessel is securely anchored. It hadn't occurred to me that the ocean is too deep to anchor in. I remember standing in West Marine debating how much anchor chain we should purchase. Based on the boat's windage and weight, we settled on 200 feet. I bring that up.

"We have 200 feet of anchor chain," I said then, still not registering that we aren't going to be resting together, *ever*, while we're underway. We'll always be literal ships passing in the night. He waits for me to do some math. For it to click.

"So . . . yeah, the ocean is deeper than that."

I agreed to the midnight shift. I learned that solo sailors set alarms every fifteen to thirty minutes to wake themselves up to check on everything. Since there are two of us, we'll get longer, uninterrupted stretches of sleep taking shifts.

When relieving each other from our shifts, we offer a quick rundown of the windspeed, the point of sail, and anything that may have broken or become cranky in the past few hours. "You've got this," Kallan says, yawning, and heads down below. The waves rock our boat, and with sails full of wind, *Seas Hope* heads south. I snuggle closer into myself: *You've got this. You are here. You are safe. You are alive.*

> Journal entry (December 1, 2017): *On the ocean. There is no one out here to make me feel guilty, unworthy, small, or unnoticed. We're all just here. Nobody is arranging their lives around "not rocking the boat."*

I am more aware of time passing during daytime sails, where I can watch the sun make its arc over us. After coffee and sunrise, and whenever my tummy calls, I make breakfast while Kallan sleeps. Chop up some onions and peppers. Turn on the gas, pull out a pan, and crack open some eggs. I hold the pan in place over the flame so that it doesn't slide with the motion of the vessel on the waves. I push the omelet onto a plate and set it on the table, then I toast some buttered bread in the pan and set it next to the eggs. On land, I never made time to make myself an omelet before heading into work. I delight in every bite.

A few hours later, a rested Kallan rejoins me. He grabs the breakfast I left for him and finds me reading at the helm seat, my book pages splashed with saltwater. We don't plan our day, we simply move through it—minute by minute, nautical mile by nautical mile. We fish, we talk, we read, we nap. We adjust the sails as the wind changes. We tinker inside of the boat. Every now and then, I excuse myself to go to the bathroom. The bathroom. It's important to pause here to talk about the bathroom.

Before we left, I remember Kallan telling me over and over again that "hundreds of men die each year falling off of boats while they're peeing over the side." He never provided the source of that information—most likely it attached itself to maritime folklore as a precautionary tale, like if you catch sight of the *Flying Dutchman* (a phantom ship doomed to sail the seven seas forever), you are ill-fated. Folklore or not, it is a valid concern and one that Kallan and I take seriously. I always head down below to the safety of the enclosed bathroom. Kallan does too in rough seas or whenever "number two" beckons. But the bathroom brings about new habits for the both of us: whether it be Kallan making sure he has a firm handhold when "going" over the side or having to put toilet paper in a trashcan next to the toilet in order to avoid clogged pipes, a bathroom experience while riding up and down waves is a wholly different know-how. Neither one of us want to experience a different version of a "Flying Dutchman" should a rogue wave catch us with our pants down.

Around noon, the sun is overhead our vessel. We prepare lunch and eat outside, watching the waves push us along. If we get really bored, we can watch *Jaws* on my laptop—the only movie I downloaded before leaving land.

"Really? *Jaws*? This is the one movie you chose to download . . . while we're living on the open ocean . . . with sharks?" I shrug. It's my favorite.

But the vast ocean and sky captivate us so entirely that we forget all about movies. Eventually, the sun starts to make its journey downward and we prepare dinner together. The sky turns a deep, fiery red.

"Red sky at night, sailor's delight. Red sky in morning, sailor's warning," Kallan says, coming up behind me to kiss my neck.

"What does that mean?"

"Weather lore," Kallan says, then explains: "We're seeing red as the sun sets—that means we should expect smooth sailing tomorrow." I learn that red wavelengths are the longest in the color spectrum, and if we're seeing them, it means they are breaking through the atmosphere of either dust particles or moisture particles. If you see red at night, it means the light is traveling through a high-pressure system (good weather) and stable air is coming. If you see a red sky in the morning, however, this could mean the high-pressure system has already passed, and a low-pressure system (a storm) may move through. Sailors should expect rain and winds. I love when he talks sea captain to me.

"We're out here," he says, his hands running down my arms. Kissing. Kisses. Everywhere.

"We're out here."

***

Night shift. Salty breeze pushes the hair from my eyes. A dolphin swims along beside us for over an hour, popping in and out of the water, her puffs of breath alerting me to her presence. Kallan pulled the sails down for the night since I'm still a newbie and the wind had picked up. We can motor for a few hours while he catches some sleep. Now it's just me, our boat—whom I'm still learning to trust—the wind, the waves, and the colossal moon. I stare at her, unable to look away. *Has the moon always been this big?* I have never looked at her in such an intimate, exposed way before. Our relationship on land was framed by my bedroom window and she was somewhere far, far off, worried about someone or something else. Now, she seems to be watching only me. Calling to me. Out here. Alone. She's so hefty. I can see her ridges and she won't stop focusing on me. I fidget with uneasiness—I'm not used to being so noticed, so silently called upon. She moves to my right. *Weird . . . does the moon move when she's out here on the water? I've never seen her move on land.* I twist my neck to follow her. *She's definitely moving.* I watch as she circles me. *Seriously. The moon doesn't rotate, does she?* I suddenly wish I had paid more attention in science classes instead of trying on the last names of boys I thought I'd marry.

She is staring at me and hasn't blinked. I watch her complete another somewhat rapid circle, my body spiraling from the neck until I've made a full rotation. *Who do I trust here? Myself? Her? I'm pretty sure moons don't do this.* Something seems off. I distinctly remember that if the sun or, I guess, the moon does a complete rotation—which she has—that means an entire day of life has passed, right? *Has an entire day of life passed!?* I wake Kallan. "Something weird is happening with the moon," I say, shaking him. "She's moving in circles."

"The moon?" He grumbles and rolls out of bed. He takes one look around and says, "The *boat* is going in circles." Somehow the autopilot kicked itself off. We've been motoring in circles for, well, at least three rotations. Hard to tell when you're a boat novice and you're surrounded by nothing but darkness.

So she hadn't been taunting me; she was trying to guide me, provide me with information, clue me in. If I had been listening with the right ears, I would have heard her say, "Trust me. I have so much to teach you."

Kallan turns the autopilot back on and heads back down to find sleep again. I shrug off the incident—a beginner's mistake—and go back to my staring contest with the moon, who still hasn't blinked. When the sun rises in the morning, we see red. *Sailors' warning.*

Seas Hope jolts and shudders. I am thrown awake. My body fills with adrenaline as I jump out of bed. Out of nowhere, forty-plus-knot gusts of wind press heavy into our sails. *Seas Hope* shakes, cries out against the force. I run outside, nearly colliding with Kallan who is running to wake me up.

"We have to take the mainsail down *now,*" he yells above the wind. Our "user's manual" (in French) states that should we find ourselves in any wind above twenty-five knots,[3] we should reduce sail. Too much wind could blow our mast down, and dismasting would be game over for our sailing expedition. It could puncture the hulls and leave us in a dangerous situation. "Welcome to the graveyard of the Atlantic!" he says and heads toward the sail. According to the Beaufort wind scale, forty-one to forty-seven knots of wind is considered a "strong gale," with effects described as: "Slight damage occurs to buildings, shingles are blown off of roofs. High waves (6 meters), rolling seas, dense foam, blowing spray reduces visibility." There is no time to be nervous or argue

3. "Knots" represent "nautical miles"—6,080 feet, as opposed to a statute (land) mile of 5,280 feet. In the days before electronic navigation, mariners would calculate a vessel's speed by counting the number of knots that unspooled from a line dragged in the water.

about how I'm not ready for this due to my lack of sailing knowledge. Ready or not, this is where I am. Bravery rises within me. I run to the helm without needing to be given a plan. My muscles engage. I turn the bow of the boat 180 degrees into the wind, thankful she's able to respond with the help of engine power. The bow raises high into the air—all sky and moon—on the upside of a wave, and then drops—a twelve-foot free fall into a dark, angry sea.

I keep my focus—eyes squinting in the wind— holding the boat on course against the crashing swell. *Come on, girl . . . come around . . . it will all be OK soon . . .* waves splash over the railings, soaking our bodies with cold December ocean. *Come on, girl . . . come around.*

Kallan, tethered in, pulls on the gigantic sail as it fights him, caught up in the wind. Feet slipping, he keeps clawing himself back to pull at the sail as water splashes around us. I keep my eyes on him. *Please do not go over. . . please do not go over . . . .*

The reality that someone could *go overboard* hadn't hit me until I watched Kallan's feet slip and his body slide from the slippery wetness of the waves. We had vaguely talked about "man overboard" protocol on some practice sails and had purchased locator beacons for our life vests, but the thought of Kallan slipping off this huge, struggling vessel in large seas in the darkness of the early morning scares me, so I avoid thinking about it. The stories I'd heard of couples leaving together only to have one of them pull into port—the other "lost at sea"—suddenly feels too close to reality.

After this night, I will struggle to sleep when I'm not on shift for quite a while. I find myself jolting awake multiple times a night, every time I hear *any* sound.

"LOVE!?"

"I'm here!"

He occasionally does the same thing when I'm on shift. How horrible it would be to awaken, rested, to find yourself alone on an empty vessel with no swimming or even dead, floating body in sight. I push these thoughts out of my head and focus my eyes on Kallan, should he fall off. He is yanking on the sail.

And then—silence.

The fight is over.

The sail is down. The wind blows past us now, as if we aren't even out here.

Kallan looks at me.

I look at him.

We exhale.

Relief washes over us.

Seas Hope breathes.

I return the bow of the boat to its original heading.

Calm returns.

We hug each other.

Frying Pan Shoals isn't taking this vessel, after all.

***

We've been offshore for days now, twenty-five miles from land and one thousand plus feet above the sea bottom, with sharks, howling winds, unpredictable squalls—and no cell service. There's no difference between us and the empty soup can floating next to us. We're all out here floating agenda-less, unsure of where we'll land, with no need to know the time, day, month, or year. My body fidgets from the freedom, the anonymity, the directionless expanse of it all.

I think back to something an old sailor told me before we left: "First comes the struggle, then the release." I made it through the struggle of leaving, and now I'm starting to feel a new tug of war: the work of being here. My body is adjusting to full-time sea living. I've sprung my sea legs. I can cook while standing with my legs spread wide to absorb any shock. I've adjusted to the watch schedules, but my body is simultaneously processing the loss of civilization and constant contact. Instead of downloading PDF files, I download a domain of boundless wilderness, and yet here I am yearning for my phone to buzz.

I received my first cellphone at the age of sixteen, the same time I received my license to drive. Since then, I haven't slept without my cellphone turned on and within reach. My cellphone stood with me through my awkward high school years, my discovery college years, my post-graduate corporate law days, my graduate school days, and even now it's still a friend—always willing to listen. It's my mother's voice when I need it; it's my girlfriend's laughter; it's my grandfather's wisdom; it's my recipe book. It produces what or whom I need, whenever I need it, with a simple push of a button. As my gateway to social media, it provides immediate feel-good feedback when I need it. To be cut off from this powerful, seductive force so built into my being? It physically hurts. It's starting to get to me. I'm itchy. *What do I have if I don't have cell service?*

The answers are all around me.

Nature. *I wonder what e-mails I have . . .*

Myself. *I wonder what other people are doing . . .*

A boyfriend. *This would make a cool update . . .*

Books. *I wonder how many notifications I have . . .*

What did old-school mariners do—those who sailed before engines made up for lack of wind, who spent months *just floating,* praying for wind to push them to their destination and relieve them from boredom? When there's little to stave off a profusion of time, silence, and nothing-expected-of-you-to-do-ness, you're left with you, yourself . . . and . . . you. I'm here stringing beads into a bracelet just because. I have time. I need a distraction from all of this.

Distraction from what, Sheena?

Time from what? Time for what? Nature? Myself? My partner? Time I've been given to exist on this Earth? As part of it instead of separate from it? I set the beads down and stare at the ocean. The beads roll back and forth on the table with the sway of the boat.

Before we left, I made a personal goal to practice yoga and meditate every morning on the boat. But every morning, instead of rolling out my mat and slowly moving my body with the waves, the only things I want to move are my thumbs—to scroll through social media or peruse my e-mails. It's 6:00 a.m. and a beautiful sunrise is happening just outside but here I am, experiencing stress just by being alive with nothing expected of me to do?

Like Pavlov's dogs, I trained myself to live life according to my cellphone's dings, vibrations, and tiny red circles alerting me of something *life-changingly, critically important.* I'd stop and shut down everything around me to zero in on my phone—mid-conversation, mid-thought. Whole moments missed. I touch my phone now to see if it has anything to offer me. Zero bars. No service. It's just a clock now, in a world where time doesn't matter. *Why am I uncomfortable sitting in this moment? Am I afraid of nothing-happening?* Zero service means zero service required of me. I feel the programming of "you must be doing something to be considered valuable" melting away. It's time I give myself what I've spent too long seeking from others: permission to be valuable, valuable me. My cell phone slides off the table, and I leave it. I make it outside for the sunrise, just as the sky bursts into colors.

***

Kallan appears from down below, his hair disheveled and his skin tanned and freckled. He looks good, yummy even.

"We only have 114 gallons of drinkable water. When it runs out, it's out until it rains," Kallan explains, "—or we'll have to stop somewhere to refill the tanks."

I've never had to think about running out of water. Growing up where fresh, clean, safe water flows with the simple twist of a handle, I never had to think about pacing my use, or how my personal consumption of water impacts the amount available for everyone else. Floating in the middle of the ocean, I am suddenly aware that of our drinking water is on a *budget*. And if there's no rain forecast, 114 gallons is really all we've got. Shower? Three gallons gone each time someone showers. Boil pasta? Half a gallon gone. Coffee? 275 milliliters gone for three cups; 860 milliliters gone for eight.

To conserve our limited fresh water, we use saltwater to wash our dishes. We set our toilet pump to pull in saltwater too. Mostly, we change our behavior, and more often I find myself looking with hopeful eyes toward the sky for rain clouds.

***

How to boat shower in an effort to conserve drinkable fresh water:

Remove clothes.

Step into shower.

Turn water on for three to four seconds to wet hair and body.

Turn water off.

Put nature-friendly shampoo into the palm of your hand and smoosh into salty hair.

Turn water on for three to four seconds to remove shampoo.

Turn water off.

Put nature-friendly conditioner into the palm of your hand and smoosh into hair.

Lather "pits and slits" with nature-friendly soap.

Turn water on for three to four seconds to wash out shampoo and soap from lathered body. Get out of the shower after using only ten seconds' worth—less than one gallon—of water.

Go outside in the wind and sun to dry.

***

I stand with a piece of moldy bread in one hand and plastic packaging in the other. I throw the bread overboard. The water and waves etch away at its edges until it's gone. I look at the plastic film in my other hand. It had been used to wrap up a single apple, a fruit that already comes with its own natural packaging. *What am I going to do with this?* Plastic takes ten to a thousand years to decompose. Under federal law, it is illegal to toss garbage from a boat while you are anywhere in lakes, rivers, bays, sounds, or less than three miles offshore. When you're far, far offshore (twenty-five miles or more)—as we are now—everything but plastic can go overboard, including grey water (sink or shower water) and black water (untreated sewage). Fun fact: urine is basically sterile; it's the feces containing bacteria, pathogens, and nutrients that can cause issues for inland and coastal waters. But out where we are? Anything goes, and every time a cruise ship passes us, I wonder if they've opened the flood gates.

Boats forty feet and longer must have written waste management plans. We're forty-three feet. First, we have to know what we're throwing away: Plastic? Organic material? Chemicals? We have three dedicated buckets:

1. First one, organics. Most goes overboard if it decomposes quickly in water. If we're entering an island or foreign country, we drop organics twelve miles or more out to prevent introduction of invasive species. No glass, cardboard, paper, or tea bags should go overboard. We save these for compost or recycling.
2. Next, recyclables. We save these items to recycle in the appropriate bin that we'll eventually find on shore.
3. Finally, waste. We're talking dunnage (packing materials) and plastics (garbage bags, fishing line, cigarette butts). We wash all waste with saltwater before placing it in a waste bucket to prevent smells and bacterial growth.

> Then we drop it on shore in the appropriate, designated bin (a bin approved for use by the public or set out for traveling sailors). This refuse will end up in a landfill.

The less waste produced at sea, the easier our lives will be, because we have to carry our trash with us until we anchor and dinghy it into land. After transferring our trash onto the dinghy, we then haul it all over again to the appropriate disposal bins. This is very different from setting trash out on the curb for someone else to take care of while you're at work—making it far easier to create an endless trail of waste.

A sailor told me that in Thailand—much like putting your children on a school bus—people stand outside by their trash and wait until it's picked up. Sailing feels a lot like that; owning our "shit" motivates us to rearrange our lives to hold and haul less of it. It took me only a few weeks of carrying waste—sometimes for miles—before I realized there was a lot of literal and metaphorical shit that I could cut out for good.

***

Before leaving home, I canceled my car insurance, health insurance, Netflix, Hulu, Amazon Prime, and electricity. The health insurance was by far the scariest cancellation.

"You're sure you want to cancel this?" my insurance agent asked. I wasn't sure. But from what I had learned from experienced sailors in the Women Who Sail group, American insurance is definitely useless in the middle of the ocean and mostly useless internationally. I had to accept some truths, they said: If I get hurt in the middle of the ocean, I better hope it can be solved, or at least managed, by a basic first aid kit. And if an injury can't be handled by a basic first aid kit, I need to become comfortable with the idea that enduring face-melting pain or death are on the table. At least until we find the nearest shore and medical doctor.

We knew that medical options are available in other countries, but we'd need to be prepared to pay cash for services. So, we stashed cash. Should we find ourselves in a life-threatening emergency, we could pull our emergency beacon, which would prompt emergency-response services to come to us. But pulling that beacon means we agree to sink the boat once rescued so that it isn't left floating unmanned. That would mean some level of temporary financial ruin. In fact, the woman who created Women Who Sail had pulled the emergency beacon in 2014 when she, her husband, and two daughters were saved from their sailboat, *Rebel Heart*. Her one-year-old became seriously ill on an ocean crossing, and the rescue mission cost taxpayers around $663,000. While they weren't required to pay for the rescue ("The Coast Guard doesn't charge," said Petty Officer Third Class Loumania Stewart, a spokeswoman for the Coast Guard division that coordinated the Pacific rescue), they did lose their floating home and all of their possessions in it.

Another very real option, I could just be OK with death; accept that it's my time. I struggled with this option the most, but I found many sailors who take this approach. I canceled my insurance, not completely comfortable with the reality of all this, but I knew my personal truths: I wouldn't be able to afford the monthly payment; since I would be out of the country, I didn't have to pay the fee for no health coverage (I would be living as a temporary expatriate); I would be extra aware of my surroundings in an effort to avoid injury. And the real big truth: health insurance doesn't actually prevent anyone from dying.

After canceling health insurance, I didn't have another thought or fear of living without it. But I do miss electricity. My disconnection from the always-available, easily accessible grid doesn't hit me until my first day in the middle of the ocean when I need to charge my laptop, iPad, and cell phone at the same time on a cloudy day.

"Pick one," Kallan says, looking at the battery bank status indicator. "We're hovering around fifty-three percent The refrigerator requires twelve percent, and there probably won't be a lot of sun today."

I pray for sun.

Chapter Seven

Finding New

I peruse the books in our shelves. We have an extensive library, thanks to my dog-hungry reading appetite as well as my inability to part with my books even when moving onto a boat. "The boat will move faster if it's lighter, you know," Kallan said when we were moving onboard.

When we're sailing offshore—as we are now, heading toward South Carolina—I can finish a three-hundred-pager within forty-eight hours, especially when I have a night shift; there's nothing to see or do other than turn pages. (Note: This statement will probably get me into trouble among rule-following professional sailors. Rule 5: always keep a proper lookout.[4] A professional, however, I was not, and I sailed off without knowing anything of Rule 5, or any rules for that matter). Now, I settle into books of maritime travel. Humans have records of waterborne vessels dating back to the fourth millennium BCE, but records indicate sea voyages started around one thousand years later, in the third millennium BCE. Thousands of years designing, testing, and redesigning vessels—all of the sharp minds and brave bodies that dedicated their lifetimes to learning the art and science of sea travel. It was their life, and now it's my new life. As the sun warms my body, I let stories of times past wash over me. I drift. When there is nothing to dodge for miles in every direction, the body eases into a deep

4. There are thirty-eight navigational rules set out by the U.S. Coast Guard. There is also the Convention on the International Regulations for Preventing Collisions at Sea, which establishes the "rules of the road." I didn't know any of these before I left but ended up learning many of them as I drifted along.

rest; the waves, with their rhythmic knocking on the hulls, pull at our eyelids. I sleep, held by the ocean.

Our vessel feels as if she's the center of all things, waves stretching out in every direction from the boat like rays from the sun. But—pull one's vision out further—and we are not the center of all things. We are a speck: of life, of time. Our vessel is a glass marble rolling along an outstretched silk scarf. Sometimes we move forward, and sometimes we're hammocked, inching backward and forward depending on how the Maker holds the scarf.

Days pass on the sea. I am learning her ways, her tantrums, her peace. We arrive in Charleston, South Carolina, after the sun has set for the evening. Landing in the dark is risky in an unfamiliar harbor, but we are tired; a rest would do everyone some good. I stand on the bow with a powerful spotlight and search for the channel markers, which indicate where the water is deep enough to safely bring in a vessel.

We slowly make our way through the channel, looking for a place to anchor. After days offshore taking poundings from the waves, our bodies crave silence and stillness. We are tired, cold, and yearning for rest, but those things can't happen until we safely secure *Seas Hope* to the bottom. *Please let us find a place to anchor. Please let us find a place to anch—*

While moving my light slowly back and forth, I see—almost too late—the mast of a sunken boat sticking out from the water. We are headed directly toward it.

"REVERSE!" I yell back to Kallan.

Without questioning me, Kallan throws the throttles in reverse. I feel *Seas Hope* jolt underneath my feet, the sudden change of direction registering in my knees. A narrow miss. I place the light beam on the mast sticking out of the water for Kallan to see. Underneath that mast lies the boat that would surely have sunk us had we hit her straight on.

"Good eyes. Good eyes," he says, relieved.

We shift directions, monitoring depths, scanning for anchored (and sunken) boats. Kallan and I assess the wind direction and speed, the depth of the water, the direction of the current, the times of high and low tides, and the distance between our boat and others. All the boats will swing in large circles around their anchors when the wind or current shifts. Boats at anchor and boats on moorings make different-sized circles, so calculating is a lot like imagining the composition of an art project. For the safety of our vessel and our lives, we cannot permit exhaustion to lull us into a quick decision. At 3:00 a.m., we find a secure place and drop anchor.

Sleep swallows us.

***

> Journal entry: *"The wind keeps pulling my hair from its tight-woven braid . . . a sign to stop regathering it all again and again. Stop forcing it back—controlled—a way different than nature desires."*

Sleeping in.

Rocking.

Quiet.

Stillness.

Traffic honks in the distance.

A train chugs off to somewhere.

But—and this is new—none of this urgency applies to me. My eyes blink open. A sunbeam reflecting off the water stretches across our sleeping quarters. I stretch.

"Hi," Kallan says, cuddling into me. He is warm; his skin is soft. I delight in his closeness after being on different shifts. Waking up has changed for me. I thought my body was waking up with the sunrise due to our assigned watch schedules, but after weeks of consistently waking up at dawn, I realize my natural clock has adjusted without any mandates from me. My new circadian rhythm feels earth-designed. I sleep when the sun goes down. I rise when the sun reappears—no alarm clock necessary.

It's still December, and overnight Charleston experienced a thirty-five-degree temperature drop. Our bodies intertwined, we still shiver in the forty-five-degree air. We don't have heat aboard our boat, so we cuddle together, prepare hot drinks and foods, or exercise. Room-temperature, or forty-five degrees—blankets help very little. When we speak, our breath leaves a misty trail.

Charleston offers our first opportunity to dinghy in and offload the non-compostable trash we've collected since we left Norfolk. I hop into the dinghy first, then Kallan passes over two full trash bags. I plunk it down next to me and the dinghy leans with the additional weight. This hunting-for-a-trashcan adventure involves stamina, time, and distance. Kallan carries one, and I carry the other. My hands and shoulders ache from the cold and the carrying. We have to find a public trashcan that's empty enough to accept our haul and then scurry off to find heat and Wi-Fi. We find one and offload.

Ashore, land-dwelling friends offer heated homes, guest rooms with cozy blankets, kitchens with warm food, showers with hot water, and laundry rooms. When you're freezing on open water in clothes that haven't been washed for a while, these indulgences are pure elegance. We accept an invitation, gather our dirty and semi-frozen clothes, and make our way to the safe haven of Kallan's friends' home.

I push dirty clothes into the washer and pour liquid soap into the washing machine.

It's the middle of a work week. Our friends have jobs and life commitments to tackle. For us, society's obligations have paused. The only thing I have to do today is warm my body and fold our clean laundry. Kallan and I sit in their sunroom and debrief about our sailing thus far.

"What's your favorite part so far?" he asks, scooting closer to me, sharing his blanket with me.

"The moon . . . the openness . . . the freedom."

"Isn't it great?"

I rest my head on his shoulder. What a gift Kallan has given me: a new way to feel about living. I no longer have to experience rush or hurry in the way land-dwellers do. No deadlines. No phone calls to return. I struggle to imagine something I should be worried about or something I "have to do." I close my eyes and listen to the sloshing of the washing machine tossing my clothes around. Soapy water pulls the salt and sweat from its fibers.

I am changing.

Something is being pulled from my fibers.

We visit with Kallan's friends each night, friends we most likely wouldn't have been able to visit at length in our previous land-dwelling lives, but when you stumble upon their city while sailing, you have time to stop—if they do—and catch up on years of life lived.

Eventually the temperature crawls to more comfortable numbers; it is time we move on. We pack up the vessel, our clothes smelling of artificial wildflowers—chemical lilacs. Kallan hugs his friends, thanking them for the gift of reprieve. We wave goodbye to our land-dwelling friends with their landlubbing lives, and point *Seas Hope* toward the ocean. The ocean itself lies on the other side of a cut known by sailors for its rushing waters and tight quarters. We can't hoist our sails due to the overhanging trees, so we depend on our twenty-year-old engines to reckon with the temperamental waters.

"Hang in there, girl," I hear Kallan whisper under his breath. We stand cadaverously still, but ready to jolt into motion should the need arise; both staring straight ahead. The four-knot current rushing against us means we are only moving at one knot under engine power. Any sudden rush of water would overpower us and push our boat backward or onto one of the sides of the tight cut we're squeezing through. We hold our breath. There's no room to turn the boat around, no way to stop. The current increases. Kallan pushes down on the lever to increase the engine power. Clanks and bangs lurch the boat forward. Our engine can only take so much. Suddenly, we're clear!

Water near the shore is more disordered than out in open ocean. It's shallower near land, so water has to bang its way around land masses and cuts. Today, it's windy and the ocean looks upset. Making it out to deeper waters will take some work.

Bang! Bang! Waves come at us—one after the other—hitting us hard. "We're going to lose the paddle board!" Kallan yells, tethering his body in. I run to the helm. *What happens if he falls off the boat even with the tether? Will he be dragged? Drowned while dragged? Dragged while drowned?* I expel these thoughts from my mind. We just have to make it to deeper water. There is a flurry of adjustments, but we stop because sometimes—this time—what's most important right now is riding it out; eventually we'll reach more depth and with depth comes calm. Kallan and I are holding onto *Seas Hope*, who's taking the brunt of it for us; we just receive the splashes. Then . . . depth. The water smooths herself out, and the boat, in response, calms. We relax into our open ocean routines.

Days pass. We no longer track the passage of time with minutes or hours, only with sunrises and sunsets.

I look forward to the moonrises. I celebrate when I see her edge peeking over the horizon. We don't talk to each other, but she has a lot to say, so I practice listening. I watch her rise and send slivers of light onto each of the waves. I like how she spreads herself, how fearlessly she assumes her space.

In the open ocean, water is free to move about, not forced into cuts, pushed around by sandbanks, or diverted into man-made lakes. The moon isn't a caricature, forced into a nursery rhyme. Out here, everyone's allowed to be as they want. No one, including myself, is incentivized to be anything they're not. "Please be you," everything seems to resonate. *Seas Hope* floats her way toward Florida. Books are read, meals prepared, charts reviewed, sails adjusted, sun absorbed, fish pulled in. Our galley's table sees fresh sushi, laughter, lovemaking. The sun goes up and the sun goes down. It's easy to forget that there's land somewhere out there, pulsating with problems. Out here there is no use for a harsh inner critic, black-and-white thinking of something being "all good" or "all bad," feelings of unworthiness, obsessive worry, chronic urgency, perfectionism, or self-abandonment. I sit reading in the sun on the bow, and the dolphins rise up from the waters to greet me. A splash of water lands on my arm, so I glance, turning my arm over in the sun: I am tanned—something I never thought I could be. We float south, dazed for days.

Watching the GPS screen, you eventually see land moving closer. Much like pulling off the interstate, we choose an exit: at which city, land mass, or island we'd like to make our next rest stop. We've chosen Palm Beach Inlet. We usually aim to arrive during sunlit hours for better visibility, but sometimes the wind pushes us faster than expected and we arrive earlier than anticipated. Navigation predicts we'll arrive at 3:00 a.m., two hours before sunrise. Sure enough, as predicted, we arrive just outside of where we need to enter the inlet in the wee hours of the morning, darkness cloaking everything. The plan is to hang out here until the sun rises, but the wind and waves are wild. We both have the hoods of our foul-weather gear pulled over our heads as splashes of waves reach over the sides of our vessel.

"It's too rough to stay out here," Kallan yells over the wind. "We'll have to try for the entrance in the dark." Covered in salt, I grab the flashlight and run to the bow.

We approach at a wide angle, compensating for waves pushing us sideways every few seconds. If we calculate correctly, we'll end up in the channel where we need to be at the exact moment we need to be there. I hold on to the railings and ride the waves up and down. *Splash.* "You OK?" I hear Kallan yell, his voice carried by the wind. I hold up my thumb, lit by the flashlight. *Yarr!* We make it into Palm Beach and anchor. Adrenaline rushing through me, I grab my journal: *"I am learning how small I am; how capable I am. I am learning nature suffers too, and she heals. How magnificent we each are. 'I'll try to explain the infinite: How rare and beautiful it is to even exist.'—Sleeping at Last." ". . . so you shall have to understand—this is the shape that I am." —David Gate*

Then we fall, cuddled and proud of ourselves, into deep, deep sleep.

CHAPTER EIGHT

Finding My Heart

We wake up to the hammering of rain—a storm passing through. Kallan dives into the water to check the security of our anchor; nobody wants the surprise of an anchor dislodging and a vessel being thrown into a fellow boater.

"We're holding strong. Let's have breakfast!"

I smile—we are holding strong.

We take a few days in Palm Beach: *Seas Hope* needs a break and some repairs; our provisions need restocking. I pass over some cash for a ballet class because my body needed to work out some of the bangs and jerks from the ever-changing sea. We befriend another young boating couple and share meals together.

In the sailing world, befriending a new sailing couple is like winning the lottery. We have not only new friends who understand our way of living, but we acquire new advisors, new hands for helping on boat projects.

"How do you handle this?"

"Could you come take a look at something?"

"I'm going to run to the store—need anything from land?"

I find my heart opens instantly to water-living people because everyone here is looking out for each other. We have to; water is actively trying to sink our homes every second.

Eventually, with some input from our new friends, we carve out a new plan for departure and we're ready to head back out.

"We'll be safe. I love you." I hang up the phone with my parents. We are leaving America—right now—at 6:00 p.m. Always saying "I love you" to the people you love, *before* hanging up the phone, is something Kallan taught me. In college, an accident left him unresponsive in a hospital bed. When he woke up a week later, he vowed to always live life to the fullest *and*, most importantly, to always tell the people he loves, "I love you."

"Because you really never know," he'd say. "And I'd want 'I love you' to be the last words I say to someone." I start saying "I love you" more often.

Kallan and I have gone over and over the plan while we await favorable weather conditions. Based on our conservative prediction that we'll sail at five knots, the passage should take us offshore with the agenda to cross the Gulf Stream, pass Bimini, check in at Nassau, and anchor in Rose Island, Bahamas. We learn later that crossing from Palm Beach to Bimini is against the current. Most people would sail south of Miami and then make the fifty-mile crossing to Bimini. But non-experienced sailors (or "experience seekers" who are unsure of what's easiest or "right") are out there making water jumps every day, too. Turns out, everything starts with making a decision to try, being as smart as you possibly can about it, and hoping everything goes according to plan.

We provisioned the day before, purchasing—in bulk— rice, quinoa, eggs, breads, fruits, meats, vegetables, and coffee along with backup shampoos, conditioners, sunscreen, razors, deodorants, contact lens solutions, toilet paper, paper towels, and sauces. Dry goods are locked in a pantry. Perishable goods are Tetris-ed into our rectangular refrigerator which over-freezes at the bottom and under-refrigerates at the top, but we make it work.

The weather window opens. In the sailing world, we are known as "cruisers." This means, we don't race and we don't tempt the gods by sailing to a set *human* schedule. The gods determine the sailing schedule by giving humans either fair weather and winds or gnarly circumstances. When the gods open the weather window: fair winds and following seas! If a sailor chooses not to heed the gods' weathers, they are on their own.

I rather like the gods determining my life's pace instead of a calendar. With a forecast showing clear skies and agreeable winds, anchor's up. We exit Palm Beach Inlet just as the sun is slipping out of the sky. Experienced sailors watch us leave, shaking their heads as they're cracking open beers.

We fight the northward-flowing current crossing the Gulf Stream. I'm not yet sure of the difference between fighting a current or going the "right" way with the current. To me, it all feels like water. Eventually, the night passes, and the sun rises. I run outside and find a comfortable spot on the bow to sit topless, drifting in and out of sleep. The sun leaves its mark on my skin around the perimeter of the book that I keep placing on my tummy for each sleep. When I awake, a giant freighter is moving by us. I wave to the crew on its deck, our boat the size of a pond flea next to their Goliath.

"I bet they enjoyed that," Kallan laughs, and I suddenly remember I'm topless.

We cook dinners together—onions, peppers, garlic—*chop chop chop* in rhythm with the melodies of Frank Sinatra pouring through our speakers. Getting ever closer to the Bahamas, we leave a trail of sultry singing, onion skins, and the aroma of fresh garlic. Dolphins peek up to follow the floating restaurant and concert. I think back to the people shaking their heads at us as we left: they are missing a perfectly beautiful crossing.

Rose Island, Bahamas

At 10:00 a.m. we've rounded Bimini and are pulling up close to Nassau Paradise Island. Already boats full of tourists with white, sunscreen-lathered noses are darting about. We wave to them. Their arms reach through inflated inner tubes. Some of them sip drinks topped off with fruits and umbrellas.

"We're here," Kallan says, smiling. We find safe anchorage, grab our passports and cash, and head to shore to check in—a routine boaters must do upon entry to any new country.

"Welcome to the Bahamas," a woman says, dropping a Bahamian stamp on my passport—my first stamp of a country I came to by boat!

"We *sailed* here!" I tell her, still not believing *we sailed to another country*.

"I know," she says, staring at me with a quizzical smile. "I just checked in your boat."

"And I *survived!* Frying Pan Shoals, freezing temperatures, open ocean, the Gulf Stream, dodging coral heads—I survived all of that!"

"Uh-huh. Enjoy your time here." We head back to *Seas Hope,* raise our Bahamian courtesy flag to confirm that we've checked in, and fall into luxurious living. Vacationers jet ski around us. I notice the difference between the time they spend on vacation and the time we spend engaging in our sailing lifestyle. They hurry through their vacations, cramming every minute with paid-for, curated activities. In the same water, we are at home, preparing meals, washing clothes, and allowing our days to drift by like passing clouds. We spend Christmas exchanging seashells.

Every morning, we rise to the songs of roosters. I spend hours on my yoga mat moving with the rise and fall of the boat. On no one's timeframe but my own, surrounded by crystal clear waters, I watch as nurse sharks circle our boat. Turtles pop their curious heads from the water. I close my eyes, take in gigantic breaths, and hold them while I listen to the birds call to one another. The morning breeze touches everything, cooling my body before the heat of midday.

I remember a Sheena who—even as a certified yoga instructor—walked out of yoga classes during pranayama because breathing was infuriating. I let go of that Sheena.

I remember a Sheena who struck out at others, irritated to the point of being inconsolable. I let go of her, too.

I remember a Sheena who flipped people off in traffic, who rolled her eyes in meetings, who went to bed on countless nights full of resentment that she'd only get a few hours of rest only to have to do it all again; a Sheena who ignored the moon as "just another fact that comes with living in a solar system"; a Sheena who would "if/then" her way through manipulation to try to get someone else's love. I let go of it all. I let go.

I am here only to exist. There is no one telling me how to do that, and even *that* truth no longer feels threatening. My cell phone? I don't even know where it is most of the time. My life reflects the blues and greens of the Bahamian landscape—open, clear, light, breezy, and full of life above and below water.

The speed of everything around me shifts. I thought life was supposed to be fast—a tornado of prerequisites, requirements, expectations. It was a culture that expected of me chronic productivity, and I gave into it all: the hurry, the rush. I put all of that into my body and became a human incapable of embracing calm. But it was never me that was the problem: I can be a calm and safe place. My obsession with "get it done; push it out; turn it around" was easier to feed than to know: My only responsibility in being alive is to let myself feel everything.

Splash!

My yoga practice finished, Kallan and I don our dive masks and dive into the water to cool off. A hundred small sergeant majors—tiny blue and yellow fish—stare back at me. *Oh, hello!* I imagine I've interrupted their school time, so I try to move out of their way. Every time I swim to the right, they swim to the right. When I swim left, they swim left. I look over at Kallan; he's sergeant major-free. I lift my arms. The sergeant majors swim underneath and around me. I am engulfed.

"They love you!" he mouths, underwater.

I smile. It does feel like love—to float weightless and feel the gentle brush of the school against me. They're teaching me to take up more space; their movement augmenting my own. It's as if they're asking me, "What space do you need to be who you are? We'll protect that for you."

The Bahamas holds many firsts for me, and I scribble them nightly in my journal under the header, "First time:"

- Seeing crystal-clear water
- Swimming with pigs
- Snorkeling
- Turning thirty-two years old
- Eating beef Wellington (after denying myself red meat for fifteen-plus years)
- Petting a stingray
- Eating conch
- Swimming with sharks (during the day, when they aren't feeding)
- Watching a shark at night (feeding time) pull a slab of steak from a rope tied to our boat
- Staring down a lionfish
- Grabbing lobsters from the rocks and preparing them for dinner
- Being followed by a million sergeant majors
- Swimming through underwater caves
- Not worrying
- Not hurrying

Life is a constant stream of say-yes-and-hope-you-don't-die experiences. At Norman's Cay, I dive down to see a drug-running plane that crashed in these waters in the 1970s. The Curtiss C-46 Commando sits on the sea floor, gutted but full of sea life—urchins, algae, and coral. I swim with the fish in and out of the windows as I imagine what it looked like before it slammed into saltwater. It was found the day after the crash with two passengers still inside.

After a look around, I'm ready to head back to the boat. I poke my head above water to assess where I need to go, wave to Kallan to alert him of my return, and start swimming. I sing to myself while swimming: *You are my sunshine, my only sunshine . . . you make me happy when skies are gray!* My arms lift in and out of the water; my flippers flip along. I poke my head out of the water to re-assess. I am . . . somewhat closer. Back under I go: *You are my sunshine, my only sunshine . . . you make me happy when skies are gray!* I poke my head out of the water again. I am starting to feel tired. I am not closer. *Am I farther from the boat?* I dive and keep kicking. *You'll get there, Sheena.*

Just keep swimming, just keep swimming, swimming, swimming, swimming, swimming, I tell myself in my best Dory voice. When I poke my head up again, I am farther away.

A mean current is pushing me away from my destination, carrying my now-exhausted body out to sea. A flipper falls off my foot. I stop swimming and reach down to grab it before it falls to the sea floor. Now I'm farther away. I tread water and try to slow my breathing, but I'm exhausted, and my body is giving out fast. A few times, my mouth and nose dip below the water. I try to relax and let my body rest.

Drowning occurs in silence. The body doesn't have the capacity to scream for help the way people do in movies. The physical exhaustion from wrestling to keep my mouth above water while the current pushes me farther away takes my voice. The current is winning. I gather my strength, wave my arms in distress, kick my legs one last time.

"Kallan!" I say, but I'm unsure if I cried out just in my head or if my voice was strong enough to reach others' ears. I let myself slip below the surface of the water, holding my breath, resting my muscles.

Kallan sees my body sinking. He jumps into the dinghy and steers in my direction. A stranger on a nearby boat jumps on a paddle board and heads toward me. I am so tired . . . *Float on your back,* a voice from my childhood says. I kick until I'm re-surfaced and make my way to my back. In a free float—no energy being used to fight the current—I'm being pushed out to the open ocean, fast. The stranger on the paddle board reaches me first. I extend my shaking arm.

"I've got you," she says. We pull my body onto the paddleboard, and I attempt to collect my breathing into some useful, recognizable pattern. Now the current is taking both of us and the paddle board out to sea, but at least my body can rest and breathe. Kallan arrives from farther away with the dinghy, which has an engine to combat the current. He throws out a line to us and the stranger holds the line: the dinghy pulls us to safety. My body slinks.

Back at the boat, I am wrapped in a towel, shivering from exhaustion and fear. Ashore, I could have called 911. Out here, it's just me, nature, and fellow adventurers watching out for each other. You have to hope they hear you cry out and have the resources available to come get you. You make trade-offs. Sometimes, they're life-and-death related.

You're alive, Sheena. You're alive, you're alive, you're alive.

***

At Thunderball Grotto, I spit into my mask, my legs hanging off the dinghy. We drop an anchor to keep our dinghy in place and push ourselves off the edge into the water.

"It's high tide," Kallan says, treading water, "so, the entrance hole is covered entirely." Now, if you're a tourist looking to enter Thunderball Grotto during high tide, they provide you diving equipment so that you don't run out of breath trying to locate and submerge yourself through the entrance. We didn't have that. Instead, we have Kallan, who says, "You just have to take a deep breath, swim straight down and look for the hole. When you find it, swim down deep enough to clear the hole; swim through to come up on the other side into the cave."

"There's air on the other side of the hole?" I imagine myself frantically pressing on the rock, trying to find an unlock button that will open the wall of rock while my breath rapidly runs out.

"Yes. When you come through the hole, the cave will open up." *I have always been waiting for my world to open up.* Head down, ass up, dive. Carve through the water. Find the hole. *Where's the hole? Where's the hole? Keep holding your breath, Sheena! Where's the hole?! Where's the hole?!*

My lungs begin to panic. There's no hole. Right as I'm about to give up and return to the surface, I see it: a circular cutout of thick stone. Low on oxygen, I push myself through, but my fear causes me to lift my head a bit. Kallan, appearing behind me, places his hand on top of my head, holding it down in an effort to keep me from smashing it on the coral.

Swim fast. Swim fast. Swim fast. Surface!

I surface inside of the cave, water dripping on my head, tropical fish eyeing me. I'm inside of a piece of earth; an underwater cave system that opens up to you after you find the small, hidden entrance. In 1965, this cave was featured in the James Bond spy film *Thunderball*, and, again, in a 1983 James Bond film, *Never Say Never Again*. Inside, naturally occurring limestone surrounds you—the sky is gone; there is only an opening that allows for life-giving sunlight to come through. Kaleidoscopes of coral appear before you like you're watching a grand choir assemble for showtime. It's a small space teeming with life, filling and un-filling with turquoise water as the tide comes and goes. Tourists holding their noses jump from slippery rocks and send the fish scattering. But the fish return, as if this is all a fun game, to prepare for their next scatter. Life is happening together: humans and sea animals; rocks and tides. I look at Kallan. I'm in awe. Of everything; of me. On my way back to the dinghy, a shark eyes my slender body. I swim, fearlessly, beside him. I reach the dinghy and lift myself from the water, exhilarated. Kallan gives me a high-five.

Georgetown, Bahamas

> Journal entry: *"The pursuit of a dream is a declaration: 'This is how I will pass my time, trade my hours, spend my energy.' It's an exchange. Every inward breath lasts until you exhale. Then it's gone, spent, a memory."*

"Good morning, boaters!" The sing-song voice of the Net announcer precedes three chimes. "The Net will begin in ten minutes!" I grab my notebook, a pen, and my coffee, and sit by the radio. The Net is a morning forum, news service, and community-announcement program connecting the three-hundred-plus boats in the harbors of Georgetown, Bahamas. Every morning the Net commences at 8:00 a.m., hosted by an experienced sailor who lives on his sailboat with a pet parrot.

The set agenda is followed every day: weather report, new arrival introductions, local business announcements, community events, giveaway/buy/sell/trade, goodbyes from exiting boats. It concludes with an inspirational quote. Not everywhere we stop has a "net." Georgetown's net is known for being the best, and it grew out of the boating community's desire to connect with other boating families floating around them.

I have a skill I want to offer to the sailing community: yoga.

Before leaving America, an old sailor asked me, "What can you offer to the sailing world?"

"I . . . uh . . . teach yoga?"

"That'll work. That skill travels. It'll give and provide." Back when he said that to me, I didn't realize he was saying that my skill, one that's easy to pack up and move around, would translate into money, goods, and services. In 21st century America, it's all swipe-swipe-swipe and deliveries left on porches. Transactions have little human aspect to them. On the water, people live less in a transactional world, and lean more into reciprocity, honoring a mutual coincidence of wants between people. Kallan, well versed in bartering, trades a hearty meal for a full day's work. Everyone's wants fulfilled. Bellies full. Friendships made. I am mesmerized.

"What do you need? What do you have?" the Net announcer asks, intro-ing the giveaway/buy/sell/trade part of the Net. *How many times have I ever been asked what I need from someone other than a restaurant server?* The kindness strikes me. The care resonates with me.

"*Seas Hope!*" I clumsily call in. What my call lacks in radio etiquette, I make up for with charisma.

"*Seas Hope*, go ahead," the Net host grants the radio waves to me.

"This is Sheena from *Seas Hope!* I'll be offering a donation-based yoga class at 9:00 a.m. this morning on the beach. Today, we'll focus on releasing tight lower backs." Then I remember the radio rule to sign off: "*Seas Hope* out." I look at Kallan.

"Now you have to teach," he says, slicing up a mango for breakfast.

I jump up and dinghy in to shore to set up. I bring my mat, my yoga music, my wireless speaker charged from the sun, and my singing bowl for meditation. I carry a hundred small shells inside each I've written "Peace," "Patience," "Hope," "Hug," "Smile," "Laughter," "Forgiveness," or "Friendship." I set the shells out on my towel and wait to see if anyone will show up.

Then, I see them—dinghy after dinghy after dinghy full of people with yoga mats or beach towels approaching the beach. Ten people. Twenty people. Thirty people. They set out their mats and towels around mine fanning out in all directions—more people than I've ever had in a yoga class on land! The different colors of people and mats turn our yoga practice into a peacock's giant, colorful tail.

"Hi, everyone. Thank you for practicing with me today."

I completed my yoga certification two years before I met Kallan, and I taught according to the book—perfectionism at its finest. But it occurs to me that I hadn't understood the philosophy of yoga until now. Sailing life is giving me opportunity after opportunity to practice trust, acceptance, permission. I extend myself boundless grace and show up to the yoga mat in whatever state of being I'm in.

The plate of shells travels around the group of yogis, each one reaching for peace, patience, hope, a hug, a smile, laughter, forgiveness, or friendship. We practice yoga together, physically focusing on releasing tension in backs compressed by sailing, but we're also practicing community, support, and self-acceptance. At the end of class, people offer their donations—cash, homemade roasted almonds, a mechanic's offer to help us fix our engine—which we really need—a necklace made of sea glass, boat-baked muffins, a Mason jar of sweet tea.

We spend a month in Georgetown making lifelong friends, spearfishing, surfing, kiteboarding. I am asked by the community to offer two yoga classes a day: one in the morning before the sun scorch, and one in the evening as the sun disappears. I also teach a philosophy of yoga class, now that I have a real-world grasp on it, to a group of homeschooled (boat schooled?) children.

"You're the yoga teacher, right?" I'm asked. While purchasing bread, eggs, and milk in the local store, a man stops me in the cold food section. I hesitate for a moment. My mind flashes back to the old sailor's question. *What do you have to offer the sailing world?* I decide to claim it, to own it, to embrace my new title within my new international community.

"I am!" I feel giddy, better than I've ever felt accepting a job offer. I am "The Yoga Teacher"—and my earnings are buying our groceries today!

"My family is coming into town tomorrow. I told them all about your classes. You'll continue to offer them, right?"

"Sure!" I say. "But we're planning to leave in a few days, so have them catch a class soon." At checkout, the cashier throws in a bag of apples.

"For your yoga," she says with a wink. I leave the grocery store, bags full of food, my heart full of pride. *The Yoga Teacher!*

The day comes for us to carry on. Through my yoga classes, we were able to reprovision, and our engines are spruced up due to hours of work provided by yoga students willing to trade their expertise. I announce our departure on the Net a day in advance.

"This is Sheena from *Seas Hope*. We are heading out tomorrow so today's class will be the farewell session." Nearly fifty people attend my class that day: boat captains new to yoga join their wives, children of all ages, locals from all over the island, and the boating community shower me with hugs, cash, and well wishes.

On the day of our departure, the Net gives me a "standing ovation"—which, in Net terms, means people click their radios on and off as if applauding. One woman who remained quiet through it all (I don't think I ever heard her speak) came on the Net and said, "I would like to offer one more 'thank you' to Sheena for her classes; they were very special." The "standing ovation" begins again. I sit by the radio with tears in my eyes.

CHAPTER NINE

Finding New Eyes

Back in the cabin aboard *Seas Hope*, we raise the sails to breathe again; they've been concealed in their covers for a month. They rustle and stretch with the wind; I can tell they're excited. Watch shifts are reestablished, and our bodies prepare for short, interrupted bursts of sleep until we arrive at our next anchorage, days away.

Sailing feels how I imagine time travel must feel: dropping in and out of moments, in and out of contact, in and out of people's lives; starting, stopping, then starting again. There are new and different rules every time you step off your vessel and onto new land. In fact, it happens that new presidents are elected while sailors are out at sea, and they return to land with entirely new leadership.

I watch the sun rise and fall as we head to a land where we'll say, "buenos días" instead of hello. In-between wind shifts, I jot down every Spanish vocabulary word I can remember as we sail toward the Dominican Republic. Days full of sun. Nights full of stars. And all the while, dolphins travel alongside until, days later, I give the signal for Kallan to drop the anchor in new land.

A large bang on the side of our boat summons us outside. A gun is hoisted onto the deck of our vessel.

"Buenos días," a large man in a military uniform says. Without asking if they may board, the man and two other gun-toting friends climb aboard. Another man who appears to be a fisherman and the owner of the boat that is now banging against our starboard side ties a line onto our boat and hops aboard.

"Papeles?" he asks, flanked by men with guns. This sends the message to us that they're ready for anything should we think "anything" is a good idea. Kallan looks at me and nods. We had discussed the possibilities of unwanted visitors, unexpected board-

ings, and requests for "tips"—so I feel prepared when he gives me the nod. I run inside and gather our passports and intake papers, showing we've paid our fees to enter the country. The large man reviews the documents, and then points up.

No flag. We haven't posted a Dominican Republic flag yet. He requires that we pay $20 to purchase a Dominican Republic flag and raise it *inmediatamente.* The flag only cost $5 at the tienda down the way, so the extra $15 is probably a blend of a tip and a tax. We pass it over—we should've put their flag up as soon as we checked in—and lift the flag. They don't leave. He sits back, arms behind his head, his feet crossed and resting on our outside table. The gun falls by his side.

"Gifts," Kallan whispers to me. "He's waiting for a tip." This time a different kind of tip—the physical gift kind. I open our pantry and grab peanut butter crackers, cookies, and, on my way out, a few cold beers from the refrigerator. I hand over the bag and watch as he opens it, thumbs its contents around, and nods his head to the other men. They rise to leave.

We find out later from an expat on his sixth rum and coke that these young military guards, wearing old, outdated uniforms purchased from the United States, are paid very little money. They have to bribe a fisherman to take them out to anchored sailing vessels, which explains the fourth, gunless guy. These small sacks of gifts are often what they take home to their families or subsist on during long shifts.

Once settled, I sit to write out a grocery list of items we need from land. From the book I read on the sail here, I learned that Christopher Columbus wrote a grocery list in 1493 while sitting only a few miles away from where I am sitting right now. His grocery list, informed by his need to feed nearly a thousand sick colonists and sent via messenger to Spain, was to be funded by King Ferdinand and Queen Isabella. It included wheat, barley, biscuit, wine (16,000 gallons), vinegar in casks, oil in jars, beans, chickpeas, lentils, bacon, beef, raisins, figs, almonds, hazelnuts, walnuts, salted fish (300 barrels), onions, garlic (5,000 strings), sugar, mustard, honey (36 gallons), molasses (10 jars), seeds, sheep and goats, calves (20), chickens (400), candied citron, sweets, dates, water scented with orange blossoms, saffron, rice, and ham.[5]

5. Laurence Bergreen, *Columbus: The Four Voyages* (New York: Penguin Group

My grocery list, not funded by Spanish royalty and intended to feed only Kallan and me, has me stumped—I don't have America's easy, go-to food options anymore. I have to re-learn how to feed myself. Since leaving America months earlier, and because we have no freezer, microwave, or oven, my relationship with food has changed. When I lived ashore, I wasn't feeding myself much. When I did, it was with dead, unhealthy, fast-and-easy, packaged, frozen, dried-out food that contained few nutrients. At the age of thirty-one, my cholesterol already tested high.

Then, I sailed away. Aisles of frozen delights or boxed-up sugar shaped into food were no longer options. New choices included: fish for protein, rainwater, vegetables from local farmers' stands, and our stock of bagged grains. After days at sea, it's time to restock our pantry, but I find myself in the Dominican Republic staring at a blank page. I scrunch up the paper and leave it on our table. *I'll figure it out off of the boat.*

When I step off our dinghy onto land, I am met by a farmer leaning on the back of his truck. He acknowledges me with a nod. I respond with a smile. A rusty scale blows back and forth, creaking from the rustle of the wind rolling in off the sea. A dog pees on the truck's front tire, which is flattened by the weight of the mountain of vegetables in the bed of the truck: peppers of varying shapes and sizes, reds, greens, yellows, and oranges; onions, layer upon layer upon layer; yucca, and carrots that twist to a point. The fruits sit next to the vegetables: pineapples, bananas, mangos, papayas.

On our sail over, I slammed my shin on the winch of our boat during heavy winds and confused seas. The boat jerked to one side and *whack!* I was on the ground, cupping my bleeding shin. *Fuuuuuuuck!* I limped back inside to clean it out with hydrogen peroxide. As the days passed, I watched the hole in my skin transform from lacerated and red to . . . bumpy, scabbed maroon to . . . peel-y pink to . . . healed. I thought back to something a science teacher once told me: "Our cells regenerate every day. Every eighty to one hundred days, you create a new, regenerated you!" With age, cells regenerate more slowly. Illnesses or complications are introduced and our bodies eventually tire and we die. But the idea that while we're living, what we eat directly impacts

(USA), Inc., 2011)

our powers of regeneration captured my interest: I have the power to create a new . . . me?

At sea, as I sat poking my healed injury one sunny day, I relished the fact that I am actively meeting a new me every day while simultaneously *making* a new cellular me every day . . . so every choice I make matters.

The foods I eat need to have their own life within them.

The images I take in need to be kind, clutter-free, relieving stress from my eyes.

The sounds I hear need to be soothing and not alarming to my ears.

The objects I feel need to be soft and sturdy.

The people around me need to feel emotionally, physically, and mentally safe.

I am changing—on a cellular level.

I remember this cellular responsibility as I fill a canvas bag of vegetables from the farmer's truck bed. I pass him two crinkly, salt-watered dollar bills, then head back to *Seas Hope* overflowing with vegetables, the raw materials I need to build a new, healthier me.

***

We hand over $14 to rent a motorcycle and two helmets, then head out to explore.

The Dominican Republic is the first country that requires me to speak a foreign-to-me language—and also to notice past wrongs, to see the parts of history my history classes never taught. Here, I recognize the marks of human intervention: land altered, water redirected, and the raucous and chaotic business of human power plays. After the arrival of Christopher Columbus in December 1492, the land and people were vulnerable to conquest and devastation. Land was rechristened, usurping the names given by Taíno natives. No matter which direction we point our motorcycle—525 years after Columbus's arrival—I feel the pain of people who were here before me and the political and financial pains of current times, the leftover sting from an unexpected smack in the face.

The coasts of the United States and the Caribbean are steeped in the horrors of slavery, colonialism, and civil war. The "cut-and-paste" version of history taught in American public schools still doesn't convey the enormity of the violence and suffering. Standing on *these* sands with *these* waters lapping at my feet, I feel complicit. The same waters that carried Columbus also carried me: how have I gotten to my mid-thirties and not known or felt the truths that come with colonization? That answer, I'm seeing now, is privilege—as well as an education design that forced people into fictional roles—slaves weren't "happy"; Columbus committed crimes to achieve what he did. Not far from where our rented motorcycle now zooms, Columbus once abandoned thirty-nine men without provisions, hoping they'd muster up a successful colony so he could return to plunder gold.

I pick a papaya from a nearby tree—something Columbus's men once did. Only then, the land had been forcibly re-named "Hispaniola" (now present-day Haiti). Historians are unsure what the Arawak/Taíno people called their island before Columbus's arrival in 1492. By 1550, the Taíno were close to extinction, knocked dead by violence and diseases gifted by the Spaniards.

Ancestral wrongdoings and communal wounds surround me, and it strikes me that I'm only now able to notice it. Vacationers at the all-inclusive oceanfront resorts (the kind of traveler I *used* to be) seem unaware, but we're anchored near a small farming town (a place no vacationers would circle on their "dream destination" maps). The reality of wrongdoings is palpable here. I imagine Columbus's boat pulling away, leaving his crew of thirty-nine men, unprepared and poorly supplied, staring at the natives. How quickly it all turned. Along with resilience and love and joy, the human spirit is capable of heartless acts in the names of power, control, and wealth. Even still, we wreak destruction on cultures, religions, and ecosystems—on people. My vision reorients.

Columbus saw land and thought "gold."

I see water and think source of life.

Columbus saw cows and thought "milk."

I see lactation and think "mothers."

I'm learning to see the world with new eyes.

"You ready?" Kallan asks over the rumble of the motorcycle. With a new spirit (thank you, Bahamas) and new eyes (thank you, Dominican Republic), I feel superpowers of consciousness, caring, capacity, and confidence rising within me. *This* is being alive.

After our motorcycle jaunt, I stand in the shower on *Seas Hope,* letting the water run down my body. Layers of engine exhaust, road dirt, coral-safe sunscreen, and sweat swirl into the drain. Layers of blindness and naiveté wash away, too.

The next day, another new vision awaits me, one I never saw coming. I wake up, and order French toast at the marina for 100 pesos. I wash my breakfast down with a glass of ice water and pay my *cuenta.* I have a chiropractor appointment in town at 2:00 p.m.—a German guy who swears he's certified. On our way to my appointment, we motorcycle to secure a *despacho,* a "ticket" of sorts, to declare our next port of entry. We visit the grocery store for *lechuga, mantequilla,* and *queso.* I stuff my groceries into my canvas bag and wave *adiós* to the locals, friends now. I stop for an ice cream and eat it quickly. The sun tries to finish it before I can. After my back is popped back into alignment (cost: $12 cash), I jump from the motorcycle into the dinghy and pull out my cellphone to check the time. We need to be out of this city by 6:00 p.m. per our *despacho.* It is 4:30 p.m.

But there is also a message from my mother: "Call me when you can." A surge of panic rises within me. One of the unspoken costs of sailing is being away from family. Receiving hard news in a place where you can't hug or help them was always a fear of mine—I had just hoped it wouldn't happen to me. "Call me when you can," I read again. I swallow the lump in my throat, force myself to wait to call until I'm back at the boat so I won't be distracted by noise or fellow cruisers who want to chat on the dingy dock. The phone rings. *Why are you ringing so slow?*

"Hello?" My mother picks up. Something is wrong. I know because she asks me ten other pointless things: "How was the chiropractor?" "What did you get at the store?" "Are you back at the boat?"

She is building herself up. She is buying time.

"Yes, I'm back at the boat." And then she tells me.

"Breast cancer—aggressive. It's serious." Shock. Anger. Blinding fear. *I thought I sailed away from everything stressful, harmful, or real. Nothing that hurts is supposed to touch me here.*

After our call, I make a salad. I grab the *lechuga* from my canvas bag and chop.

Chop, chop, chop.

I grab a carrot.

Chop. Chop, chop.

By the time I get to the tomato, my vision is blurred with tears. When we sailed away, I assumed I had left my challenges behind. Struggle in paradise doesn't compute. Kallan knows something is wrong. I throw a perfectly fine, half-cut tomato off the boat. The juices fly every which way. I sit down and cry.

I think of Charlie. Charlie is a tall, lean, kind man in his late sixties. His moving-toward-gray hair falls thinly around his tan and toned face. He used to work out, but then cancer settled somewhere deep inside his bones and he got tired. He sold his belongings and moved onto a sailboat anchored less than one hundred feet from ours. He flies home to Florida occasionally for treatment and dinner with his daughter, carrying with him a truth heavier than his one small duffle bag: the treatment isn't a cure; it's only buying time. Scars from failed medical intervention vine up his legs.

"I'll die alone here on my boat," Charlie told us with a contented smile. He's told this story often and each time he collects more peace with it. The local marina knows his plan. His daughter knows, too. They are always checking in; nobody wants to leave a dead body floating for too long. I'm not ready to send my mom floating down a river to heaven. I'm not ready to accept that there's no escape from hardships. A cloud of thick reality settles upon me. This isn't an untouchable "gap year." This is life.

CHAPTER TEN

Strength

Distracted, scared after the news of my mother, the deadline comes up on our *despacho,* which means we have to sail regardless of feelings. We are required by the gun-toting navy to leave the Dominican Republic by 6:00 p.m. The weather window opens to move south, so we pull up the anchor and head out.

Our boat follows weaving waters cutting through lush, jungled mountains. Monkeys roar as we leave the Dominican Republic and head toward the Mona Passage, its seas known for being treacherous and deadly. These waters are also famous for drug traffickers and mating grounds for humpback whales.

I am stuck in a blur of fright and sadness, my nose red and eyes puffy from crying. I had heard the Buddhist story:

"What does one do before enlightenment?" The novice says to the master.

"Chop wood. Carry water," replies the master.

The novice then asks, "What, then, does one do *after* enlightenment?"

"Chop wood. Carry water."

With one hand on our Bimini top for balance, I try to recalibrate myself—pre and post a cancer diagnosis. The only difference being *now you know.*

You always hold onto something when you're sailing because your body is constantly in motion. You burn calories just by sitting because your body is working to stay balanced upright. You're always anticipating where a hit can come from next—a dance of bracing yourself while remaining flexible, open to the unknown. This was me now: talking myself into a *braced flexibility*—trying to be strong for my mom and still open to life happening for me.

"Whale!" Kallan interrupts my reverie.

On deck, the wind brushes against my raw cheeks. From under the depths of the sea, a gargantuan body rises, followed by an enormous tail. Here and then gone. Gone and then here. I watch as the whale—first one and then two and then three—move like needles dragging thread, piercing up and then under, sewing the time of their lives.

"There is always something profoundly good . . . even in what's hard," Kallan whispers to me. "We're going to find the good together."

I didn't see this diagnosis coming. I didn't see this diagnosis for my mother, especially not *now* when I'm so far away. But I see now that life happens, like these whales:

We are here and then gone.

Gone and then here. The sun slips from the sky as the whales sing their songs.

***

On my night shift, I stand outside looking around. The moon is here with me, but she's just a sliver tonight; it's dark. I click on a flashlight and throw the beam around. I know it's futile, as there would be little I could do should something life-threatening pop up in the short length of my flashlight's beam. But the light offers the slightest bit of comfort.

I'm already chapters into my book. All is quiet but the waves on the hull. There's no radio chatter. Nothing. I open my book to begin chapter five. I'm two sentences in when a speeding engine rushes by—close by—our vessel. I drop my book and run outside. I hear the engine moving farther away; it's definitely speeding, but I see nothing.

I stumble, trying to collect my flashlight, find the button and click it on. By the time the shaky light beam makes its appearance, I no longer hear the engine. I swear I had just checked if anything was near us. There was nothing. I make my way back inside and pick up my thrown book.

At our shift change, I tell Kallan what I had heard. I'm positive it was an engine, and it sounded *so close*, like I could've reached my hand out and touched the passing boat.

"Most likely a drug boat," he says, pouring the coffee I had made for him.

A day later, when we refuel in Puerto Rico, a border patrolman asks if we saw or heard anything while we were underway. I relay the information about the late-night speed-by with no navigation lights to be seen. He confirms this is how drug boats transport their goods: blacked out boats speeding through the night, no lights to reveal positioning, no stopping for friendly chitchat. I later read in the newspaper that the U.S. Coast Guard of San Juan intercepted a vessel carrying 4.2 tons of cocaine. I don't know if that was the vessel that buzzed our boat, but it leaves an imprint on my memory: A magnificent place—the shimmering open ocean—goes untouched by cancer diagnoses and human crime.

***

In Puerto Rico, we get the news that my mother's surgery is scheduled with the goal to remove what they can and determine if it's spread. I spend an entire day crying in Kallan's arms trying to process conflicting feelings tangled within me: free and bound, lost and found, desirous and avoidant, careful and careless, present and absent. I process shock and tragedy against the landscape of freedom and paradise. Two things that seem like opposites can both be true. I feel my framework moving from "either/or" to "both/and," and that shift opens up a safe and flourishing place to be multiplicitous. Suddenly, this cancer diagnosis is less about life or death, and more about her life; cancer's death; the death of an old version of her giving rise to a new one; an opportunity for me to learn how to support, to listen, to love from afar, giving her the space to tell me what she needs. The cry is a gift. I realize that I can hurt surrounded by beauty. I can be soft and strong. I can carry on.

The nature around me doesn't tell me to "buck up" or that I'll be okay or that I shouldn't worry. Nature doesn't crumble when I'm crumbling. Nature whispers: "Love is for giving. Love is forgiving." Kallan holds me as we rock gently in our hammock.

During this leg of our travels—processing the diagnosis—I thought a lot about how death overtakes us, often by surprise. How if the boat springs a leak, or if a whale breaches too close to the hull, we'd be left floating on a sinking vessel. How if I fall off and Kallan can't turn the boat around fast enough then I'm left treading water until my body gives out. What it may feel like to be on the receiving end of a shark clenching down his teeth into the softness of my belly;

legs snapped, the only thing left to do is let go and sink down. In the Dominican Republic, I saw the lifeless body of a young woman who was thrown from her motorcycle. A group of people circled around her to be with her while her life slipped away. Then, her spirit gone, they left her body in the middle of the road awaiting an ambulance. I think of Charlie. I think of cancer. I think of how we'll all one day slip into a new form. Our bodies have the power to create and the power to end.

Predictable, consistent health can be taken from you by unpredictable circumstances. One's left with only one option: we must embrace the chaos of this life, the beginning, middle and end of it all, the "you-can't-control-this" of it all. We must live—*we must live*—while we're alive. After hours of crying, I am emptied, quieted, and still alive. I can carry on. I find my strength and rise from the hammock. *Acceptance. Rebirth.*

We rent a car with our friends on *Sailing Satori*—Nick and Kelly, a couple we'd met in the Dominican Republic. They crossed the Mona Passage with us, and now we've anchored close enough to swim to each other's boats for happy hours. They have a tradition of seeing a movie in every country they travel to, and since we could use a pick-me-up, we decide to join them.

At a Walmart, the first one we've seen since leaving the United States, we purchase an inflatable pool to place on the bow of our boat and fill with water to be heated by the sun. Then we search for conch and throw parties with conch salad and white wine in our makeshift hot tub. We pull each other on surfboards behind our dinghies and watch the U.S. Coast Guard run evacuation practices.

Back at home, my mom starts her own version of *Chop wood. Carry water.* She is prepped for surgery. I am with her—and also oceans away.

***

The morning sun warms my skin. Water slaps against the hulls. Our satellite phone pings. "Cancer aggressive. Doctors suggest you get a mammogram ASAP." Back to reality. Emotional whiplash. I turned off my health insurance along with my Netflix subscription. Expensive, American medical procedures were not considered when we made our sailing budget—a measly $1,000 a month for two people and an old boat.

"Morning." Kallan flips on the gas stove for coffee.

"My mom's doctors think I need to get a mammogram. Family history of cancer and . . ." my voice trails off.

"We'll find a doctor." He kisses my forehead and pulls out the map. Our next destination: a city with medical equipment.

Just like that.

Like it's nothing.

I melt from his response, his care of me. I assumed I wouldn't go to a doctor; I was just sharing information I had received via our shared satellite phone.

We sail to Humacao, Puerto Rico, and the sea is light and easy, a much-appreciated gift from Poseidon when emotions on board are on the heavy side. We pull into a marina in the late afternoon. Only eight months have passed since devastating hurricane Maria, and Puerto Rico is still recovering. Roofs are covered in blue FEMA tarps. The electricity is off. Trees refuse to bloom. "They're in shock," a local tells us. I learn later that the trees were burned by saltwater splashes, weakened by flooding, and twisted by winds. There's a rule of thumb that for every inch of caliper—the diameter of the trunk measured six inches above the soil line—it undergoes shock for one to one-and-a-half years. Larger trees suffer longer. I wonder how long the shock of cancer will resonate within my family.

"Beautiful boat!" We pull into a slip at the marina and a tall, middle-aged man wearing khaki shorts and a Hawaiian shirt tilts his afternoon drink toward us. "We wanted to buy one just like it." His hair is dusted with grays. Suave and content, he's smiling and tanned. I can smell his coconutty beverage when the wind travels in the right direction.

"What brings you to Puerto Rico?" He reaches out his hand to catch our dock line and wraps it around the cleat.

"We're on a doctor stop," Kallan explains, shifting the gears as he perfectly leads *Seas Hope* to where she needs to be.

"Everyone on board alright?" he asks, alert and ready to help if someone is in need of emergency care. A fellow sailor knows when a boat comes in off the ocean, emergent care could be a possibility and every passing minute is critical.

"We're alright. My mom was diagnosed with an aggressive form of breast cancer back home. Her doctors suggested I complete some tests." I walk from the bow to the stern, checking lines and bumpers.

"Hold on." He pulls out his cellphone.

I wipe beads of sweat from my forehead and watch him walk down the dock toward a Lagoon catamaran named *Dagny T*, a character from the novel *Atlas Shrugged*. His boat, we later find out. We can't hear his hushed voice over the slapping of the water around the pylons. Within minutes his wife appears on the dock. The couple stands side by side. We haven't set a foot down on land and already we have two new friends.

"We can help you," she says. She has had her own tango with cancer.

Kallan looks over at me. The universe is taking care of us. And I know he's right.

Tom and Anne-Marie, boat lovers and island-life lovers, moved from the mainland to Puerto Rico to run their own financial advisory business: "Who wouldn't want to work looking at . . ." They hold their arms up encapsulating the postcard-perfect island views. When the hurricane slammed into the island, it supercharged their already innate desire to help others. Their caring hearts are boundless, we soon learn. Since the storm, they have been all-hands-on-deck helping people in need.

Their neighbor happens to be a doctor—their doctor. Text messages are sent, and a doctor's appointment is scheduled for me, all while I'm tying a wrap skirt around my waist—though sailors don't mind carrying on serious conversations in nothing but swim attire.

"OK." Ann-Marie clicks her phone off and tucks it away. "You have a doctor's appointment tomorrow. Ruth will pick you up and take you."

The following morning, Ruth's car pulls up at the marina.

"Hey," she says, smiling. "Jump in!" Ruth is Anne-Marie's full-time Spanish-speaking assistant. Bouncy curls frame Ruth's smiling face, and her laugh makes you feel good. Ruth will help me ensure that nothing is lost—in traffic or in translation.

I sit in front of a doctor who balances his glasses on the very tip of his nose. I explain my mother's diagnosis and the "Mammogram, ASAP" suggestion from my mother's doctor. Ruth translates. He nods his head in agreement and sends me out with prescriptions for an ultrasound, a mammogram, and blood work.

At the lab, I let them know I have no insurance.

"No problema." The secretary clicks away on her computer and then smiles, motioning for me to take a seat. When it's my turn, a mammographer lifts my arm and cups my breast and moves it around on the cold, flat surface. She doesn't speak English and I speak very little Spanish. She smiles at me and I smile back.

"Is good?" she asks. "Small!" she says, cupping her two hands together like she was holding a wee bunny, then motions to my breast with a giggle.

My breast presses flat. I miss my mother. I have never had a mammogram before, and I never anticipated there being an ocean between us when I got my first one. I want her here with me the way she stood by me when I was a child getting my finger pricked. *"Terminada."* She points to the door as I gather my breasts back into the hospital gown.

Next is the ultrasound. Ruth sits with me, my boobs out, and translates. My results come back clean and clear.

"No concerns," the doctor says. Ruth smiles at me, and a wave of relief washes over me. I grieve for my mother who hadn't heard those words, who will begin chemotherapy any day now. We pay $150 cash to the doctor—for a mammogram, bloodwork, and an ultrasound that would have cost $2,000 back home—and I send the "all clear" message back to the states.

That night, I sit at Anne-Marie's dinner table, which overflows with rice, meats, vegetables, and wine.

"Why did you want to help me?" I ask, genuinely curious. I am a complete stranger who sailed in from the unknown. Her kindness has deeply touched my heart—and my mother's as well, who found the whole story difficult to believe when I told her on the phone.

Anne-Marie took a sip of wine. "During the hurricane, my father was very ill. I needed to return to Sweden, but no commercial planes were going out. Out of nowhere, a stranger offered me a seat on his private plane. He knew I needed help, and he knew he could offer that help."

She pauses and looks at me. "I knew you needed help, and I knew I could help you." She refills my glass. Anne-Marie lives by that simple life rule of unconditional love: when someone happens across her path in need, and she knows she specifically could help them—that is all she needs to see.

Back on *Seas Hope*, warmed with the doctor's good news and Anne-Marie's wine, I sit in the hammock strung across the stern of our vessel and stare at the moon. My mother once told me that when her mother passed away, she started seeing her face in every full moon. I look up. There they are, my mother and grandmother. I smile, comforted by their presence. This moon imbued with a stillness and grace, pregnant with wisdom and calming powers, and tonight, with the faces of my maternal lineage. They are thankful for my clean reports. I am thankful to feel connected to them.

It's time for us to sail onward. We say our goodbyes to Tom, Ann-Marie, and Ruth the next day. They stand on the dock and wave as our boat moves out of the marina, then they turn and walk away.

On my watch I notice a quickly, deeply graying sky ahead of us. The clouds are churning, and my skin registers a temperature drop. I am good at guessing windspeeds now. My skin feels first, then I guess and confirm my guess with the wind meter: 19 . . . 22 . . . 24 . . . gusts power up to 31 knots. Kallan is downstairs asleep. Not so long ago, this is when I'd usually panic and run to him to have decisions made.

With all of my effort, I pull in the jib and reef[6] the mainsail since the gusts are already beyond where our manual suggests reefing. I feel confident. I'll trust my own homegrown sailor instinct.

I still want sails up so I'll have power to steer. Fortunately, we're running downwind, being pushed into those clouds that now look a lot like rain. I close the windows and grab my foul-weather gear. *You've got this, Sheena.*

Seas Hope reaches the storm cell. The clouds open on us and large, pelting rain drops. I check everything: windspeed, the way the sails are interacting with the wind, our point of sail. I throw off my hood and let the rain hit my face. I feel it slide down my hair and cheeks. I can't keep my smile from bursting through. I am sailing. I am the captain.

Sheena, you're alive. You're alive. You're alive.

Down below, Kallan awakens and comes running out, alarmed. He looks over everything, assessing my judgment calls. I am soaked,

6. *Reefing* is a term that refers to reducing the sail area of your mainsail to prevent the sailboat from becoming increasingly difficult to handle as winds increase.

squinting through the pelting rain. Without saying a word, he looks at me, lips pursed, impressed, and retires down below, the markings of raindrops on his skin.

Well, I'll be damned you ol' sailor, you. Rain clings to my eyelashes. I loosen my hands on the wheel and howl.

CHAPTER ELEVEN

Turning Point

Before we even locate an open mooring ball, Kallan is texting old friends on-island who are awaiting our arrival. He exudes the energy of a boy returning home after being away too long. Memories of our first date come flooding back. When he explained that he once lived with, married, and loved another woman, it was here. On this island. He worked on charter boats and taught island visitors how to snorkel and dive here. He knows the bars and restaurants because they were his daily hangs. I finish tying off the line that holds us on the mooring ball. He rushes to drop the dinghy.

"I'm home," he says, arms open, bare chest to the sky. He cranks the dinghy down, inch by inch, until it reaches the turquoise water of the islands. "We made it."

As soon as we arrive in St. John, U.S. Virgin Islands, it's evident that Kallan would be content to stay forever. His family buys airline tickets for a visit. He sets up an account on Airbnb to start renting out the guest quarters on *Seas Hope* and schedules dinners—well into the future—with friends. I tag along on adventures as we hop between the U.S. Virgin Islands and the British Virgin Islands. There's a lot of beauty to entertain myself, but after three months, our opinions diverge.

"We could make some business cards and start a charter business here," he says, plopping pepperonis down on a pita pizza he's warmed with the solar oven on the bow of the boat. He says this like newly engaged couples imagine their white picket fences and 2.7 kids.

I listen, confused. "You could get a job teaching yoga, and I could bartend and run charters."

I fiddle with the rough edge of a seashell in my hand. *Am I hearing this correctly? My dreaming, free-sailing boyfriend? Talking about jobs? Business cards? Roots?*

Just around that mountain, past that bulge of land, is the ocean . . . and South America. People, foods, dancing, history, and stories of long-lost pirates beckon me. Surely we didn't uproot just to root down again a few months later. "The jump to South America won't be easy. I don't think you're ready," Kallan says, stuffing the pita pizza in his mouth.

Has my free-spirited, believer boyfriend become a naysayer—a prescriber of what I am capable or incapable of? I am aware of the facts: that the jump to South America would be the longest passage we will have undertaken so far, and that there are only two of us to make the jump. But the jump feels feasible—if you want it enough.

I pull off my coverup and dive into the water. Every time I come up for air, I hear his reasons for settling down.

"We'd have a lot of support here." The coolness of the water washes over me. "We'd make great money, too!" I sink below the water line. *Can I hold my breath long enough to drown out what I'm hearing?*

At the beginning of our journey, Kallan asked: "Why stay? Why not go?" *I* was the one who'd asked, "Why go? Why not stay?" Now we're standing on each other's old stomping grounds. My eyes are on the open ocean; Kallan is designing business cards and suggesting applying for jobs.

After months of postcard moments snorkeling, swimming with turtles, finding shells, hiking, and visiting with family and friends, here we are about to end our adventure and, quite possibly, our relationship. I have no interest in settling down here, and he feels called to. Not only is Kallan settling in, but the universe seems to be testing me, too. Every time we're on island I find my email inbox full of invitations to put roots back into the ground.

A freelance writing contract offer: *Think about the money.*

My mom's cancer: *Think about your family.*

A friend's wedding: *You can't recreate major life events later.*

A new nephew: *He'll only be this little for so long.*

"I want to keep going," I say popping up from the water. "There's more of the world to see." He stares at me, swallowing a large bite of food.

It hadn't occurred to either of us: we're different people now. The reality of this enters us the way water enters a small crack in a vessel—slowly at first, eventually rushing in. It occurs to me that maybe we *had* done all of this just to return here. Maybe here, in his mind, is where his personal legend ends.

But my own personal legend is starting to sharpen its form, and I'm bold enough to claim it now. I can see and feel it more clearly the more my inhibitions fall away, the more I trust the world around me, the more I manifest my desires to live fully—all skills I awakened thanks to him. My personal legend is just beginning its alchemical transformation; it isn't meant to stop here. If I stop now, I'll be shorting the lessons the universe has waiting for me. Up until now, this has been Kallan's journey, and I've been a trusty but passive first mate. I've pulled the lines I was directed to pull. But now I'm capable of choosing which lines I want to pull and where I want to head.

"It won't be a smooth or easy jump," he warns.

"I can do it." I pull myself up onto the boat, wrap myself in a towel, and kiss his cheek. Inside, I crack open a beer.

While refusing the resignation letter of an exasperated Secretary of State John Hay, President William McKinley said to him, "We must bear the atmosphere of the hour. It will pass away." I think of this line from David McCullough's *The Path Between the Seas* as we try to sort through our differences in limited space. *Bear the atmosphere. It will pass.* Twenty-four/seven intimacy is our only scenario, and this can feel like being wrapped in the comfort of your favorite blanket or like being attacked *everywhere* by biting fire ants. We learn to move between the two extremes. We bear the atmosphere and the time it takes for us to work through our differences and find each other again.

Nick and Kelly of *Sailing Satori* have stuck with us since the Dominican Republic, and I beg Kelly to join me for a pedicure one day, just to breathe. She and Nick have a path they seem to agree on: when the time is right for them, they'll move the boat back north. They'll spend hurricane season in the Dominican Republic and afterwards, sail back to Florida.

Kallan and I remain uncompromising. We want different things. If we had been honest with each other and with ourselves, we'd have known we wanted different things from day one, but full-time travel has a way of acting like Saharan dust. It coats everything until whatever you're looking at has become a different color. Plus, we aren't ready to give up on each other yet. It seems we are quietly asking ourselves: "How do we stay connected?" I squeeze his hand as he walks by in stubborn silence: a small act of hope to say, "I'm still in here. I'm still for you, for us." He returns the squeeze, and my body relaxes.

The boat has a long, ever-growing list of not-working necessities that also make our lives increasingly difficult. We've been out cruising for half a year, and the boat has taken some hits. Bolts have rattled loose. Lines have begun to unravel. Our port engine decides which days it wants to work. It's been six months since we've had real showers or felt warm clothes come out of a dryer, but that doesn't bother me anymore. My hair has gone full wild, and my body has adapted to living without air conditioning. But tension augments tension, and Kallan and I find ourselves repeatedly having to swim upstream to get back to each other.

Time passes. Hurricane season is creeping up on everyone and the stories of hurricanes Irma and Maria still cling to everyone's lips. Happy hour conversations with other boaters become a little less happy when the inevitable question comes up: "Where are you guys riding out the season?"

"We're still figuring that out," one of us says. We're coming closer and closer to needing to make that decision. Discussions of money, plans, jobs, and responsibilities make the freedom we fought so hard for feel *restrained*. I think of my gas-station muffin. What difference is a gas-station muffin here versus where we left? A gas-station muffin surrounded by clear blue waters? I can't pinpoint what is wrong. *Is it me? Is it him? Is it us?*

On an evening when I need a break from the atmosphere, I swim to shore. A couple vacationing from Washington, D.C. notices that I swim in from my anchored boat. Questions about boat life pour out of them. I find myself only able to vent the nonromantic parts of it all while gnats gnaw at my legs.

"I thought we left the rat race to sail away, and now it seems he wants to pull the uniforms back on again—clocking in and out. Pulling a shift. Just to, what? Say we live on a boat that's anchored to the sea floor while our lives are still governed by a work schedule and someone else's expectations? I want to keep moving, keep trusting, keep following the wind."

"You've rewired," the woman says, "a rewiring of self." She smiles as she eyes me over the rim of her tipped-up coconut-smelling cocktail. Something tells me she knows because she once rewired herself, and now she's living on the other side of it. She's right. I have rewired.

With every new port and every sail, I've rewired myself, again and again, each time resulting in a different version of me. I'm the old me and the new me, a school of unlearning, relearning, and learning.

Glee rises within me. *You're alive. You're alive. You're alive.* I thank her for the company and then walk into the water—to swim back home—a mermaid disappearing into the water to return home. My home. My floating boat home that moves through time and space with the waves and wind. My floating home that has rewired who I am. I know clearly now that I want to keep traveling, even if that means finding ways to travel without him or his boat. I know my options now because I've seen travelers coming and going from all over the world and making it work on a shoestring budget.

As I swim back, I know exactly what I need to say to Kallan; words I once heard him tell me: "I won't stop here. I must go onward—with or without you."

> Journal entry:
> *Rewire for your sanity.*
> *Rewire for your health.*
> *Rewire for you.*

On the calendar's edge of decision-making regarding a hurricane season call, Kallan decides to roll with my desire to go south. We patch everything we can—broken boat parts and our relationship—and I let the line slip through the mooring ball. We're going. Point of sail: Bonaire, Dutch Caribbean. Then, South America.

Back out at sea. My eyes adjust again to seeing two halves: the dark navy—almost purple—waves, and the light blue of the sky. No land, bird, or building breaks the two halves. My ears relearn to accept the loud bang of the waves on the hulls and the occasional loosening and quick tightening of the open sails as the wind changes.

I am deep into the chapters of my books, starting new ones from our growing collection of port-exchanged literature. I hang my feet off the back of the boat and flip pages where salt tickles my toes when the line on our fishing rod yanks taut, screeching. I toss my book aside. Grabbing the fishing pole, I reel quickly, then stop and do a slow, elongated pull—a little something I picked up on from watching *Jaws*, the only movie I downloaded and have watched twenty-two times thus far. Giving in to full dramatics, I even find myself saying, "He's gone under the boat. He's GONE UNDER THE BOAT!" Kallan scoffs.

"I bet it's just sargassum weed." He watches the line. He leaves the fish spear untouched, confident in his nonbelief with a go-ahead-and-prove-me-right look on his face.

"It's a fish." Reel. Pull. Reel.

There's a flash of neon and blue; a thick tuna jumps into the air.

"No shit!"

I wrestle the tuna close to the boat and Kallan grabs the spear. He thrusts the blade into the tuna's flesh and a trail of blood trickles behind him. I always feel horrible right at this moment. Murderous even. But when you're out on the sea for days, the body craves, and fish is the only meat your body gets.

We clean the blood that landed on the boat by splashing it with seawater. The fish lifts our spirits, and we sing, temporarily suspending our differences. We've memorized every word of every song on our pre-downloaded sailing playlist and we sing them loudly—and naked—to the audience of clouds, floating sargassum, and passersby on cruise ships who snap photos on their iPhones and must wonder, "Why would two naked people be all the way out here on that tiny boat?"

After a topnotch fish dinner, before we settle into our late-night watch schedules, we hold our bodies tightly together. *Let's forget our differences.* We kiss salt from each other's limbs while the sky bursts into sparkles. *Rewired, the heart desires to beat.*

It takes us four days to reach Bonaire—ninety-six hours of open ocean, dolphins, and Shakespearean displays of shooting stars and rising moons. We take shifts and both pull off some great sailing.

Occasionally we run into a snag. I suggest an altered course or request that Kallan ease the Genoa lead car[7] in an effort to power

7. Jib/Genoa lead cars allow you to change the angle of your sail for a more efficient shape, resulting in better speed.

up. I want to push *Seas Hope*. Kallan will reach to spill wind[8]. I sometimes see a flash of pride in his eyes, and sometimes what feels like confusion. *Is he proud of my new voice? Or threatened?*

With every sun and moon rise, I fall deeper in love with the arrangement of things: our Earth's lineup in the solar system, the divine timing of me being where I am in the moment, the guides and teachers we've met along the way, my mother's battle with cancer progressing well, the trials of full-time sea living, the presence of sea animals who rise from the dark waters to look straight at you with what feels like infinite wisdom.

During a night watch, buried deep in a book, I hear a voice inside of me: *you should spend more time with the moon.* I don't know where the thought—or voice—comes from, but I shut my book, leave it on the chart table, and head outside. Out on the ocean alone, I have noticed her a lot more, and I've gazed at her for comfort in an attempt to feel connected to my mother and grandmother. But I have never spent quality time with the moon because she asked it of me. I've never been sensitive enough to hear her invitation. I've never had time enough to heed her call. I've certainly never been open enough to receive from her. I've only projected onto her what I desired to see.

Outside, our boat is surrounded by a heavy cloak of darkness. The only reprieve from the blackout is the moon—waxing gibbous. I walk around and sit in the helmsman's seat. I untie my hair and allow it to blow in the wind. I remove my shirt.

I am exposed.

I am calm.

I am listening.

She doesn't react. She doesn't look away. She keeps shining on me. She bathes me in her pale, colorless light as if she's dipping a cloth into her sweet light and running it slowly down my arms, legs, and the back of my neck. The washing of a body.

I turn my forearm and palm over to allow her more reach of my body. Her light moves, like the crawling of a ladybug, to the soft, inside skin of my arms.

"You have been with me since that first night out on the open ocean. I noticed you then, accused you of trickery; I'm sorry.

8. *Spilling wind* means letting out the sheets, or sails, which results in slowing the boat down.

You've only wanted to accompany me. You've been here patiently waiting for me to see and appreciate the order of things. A teacher. A mother. A guide."

It's my turn to listen. I close my eyes and listen to her stories—stories of celebration and stories of violence. She's witnessed loss and gain and countless transitions of people, societies, wars, religions; seasons, floods, animals, and storms. I am inspired by her capacity to sit back and watch, to help with the wobble but not be seduced by the urge to grab and control it. Hers is a life of simple complexity—of always having to deal with the gravity of seeing it all while powerless to alter a thing. Our boat pushes onward. I stay with her until the eastern sky brightens.

"Morning, sailor," Kallan pops his head out just as the sun is making an entrance.

It's time for me to sleep. I re-dress myself and hand over the vessel. I make myself comfortable in bed, bracing my leg against the wall so the waves don't roll me around.

What a night.

* * *

We arrive in Bonaire at dusk. After days at sea it's always comforting to see a town. You never know if society collapsed while you were away. We set our anchor and settle in to watch the sky change. One blanket shared by two. One hot beverage shared by two.

"We made it," Kallan says, putting his arm around me. "Ya done good, kid."

We fall into a doze on the trampoline. The late morning sun warms me awake. I rub my eyes and look around for Kallan, who is bringing coffee. We chat about what broke or shifted during the sail over. He makes a mental note of replacement parts to search for on the island. The water calls with its turquoise shallows that drop off into a deep blue abyss. I slip off my clothes, dive into the crystal blue, and wade around. *Hello, abyss.* Fishes eye my naked, freckled body.

Soft corals undulate in the gentle current.

Beneath me, movement.

Above me, movement.

Within me, movement.

Kallan watches me as I swim around. I am smiling, air filling my lungs. He removes his swim trunks and joins me. Shaking his long, sun-bleached hair, he sprays me with seawater. He pulls me close, my breasts pressed against his muscular body. *We're healed, maybe, from our different grounds. We're standing, maybe, in the same place now.* We're treading water. If we remain in and under and of the water, our relationship is safe. Maybe it's just the ground that threatens to end it.

"Let's go check in." Kallan swims to the ladder.

Ground is calling.

We spend the midday hours checking in to the country and tracking down replacement parts for the boat. We find a young couple who works on sails; our mainsail is in serious need of sewing since strong winds popped its clew.[9] We yank and pull the mainsail down and hoist its heavy weight—almost like dragging a dead body—onto our dinghy. The mainsail takes all of the available sitting room, so I lie on top of it while Kallan steers the dinghy, the weight ensuring that the dinghy is traveling at all of three mph.

By the end of the day, we're physically exhausted but spiritually energized—a state completely opposite from what I used to feel on land. This is the state we're made for, I think to myself: expending our energy exploring and working for ourselves, then feeling inspired by it all at the end of each day. No energy is left unused, unspent, unnoticed.

We're ready to explore parts of the island that aren't covered with boat parts—a night out on the town! As the sun tucks itself away, I shower off the salt and pull on a bright red dress. It falls down over my body, airy, whimsical, caught by the winds. I've shed pounds and gained muscle. I've tanned, something I was told back home that a redhead would never be able to do. I hear the voice that called me outside to the moon: "Good choice, red. Red connects with the energies of life—blood, fertility, healing." I feel saucy.

As I strut down the main street of Bonaire in my red dress underneath a now-full moon, I recall my sea-surrounded moon bath. I feel new, like someone else entirely. Beside me walks a woman I met while we were both out swimming. She lives on the boat anchored next to us with her husband and aging dog.

---

9. The clew of a sail is a metal loop attached to the lower corner of a sail.

"How are you feeling?" she asks, her thin blonde hair bouncing at her shoulders. She's the same build as me—tall, lanky. She was once a dancer, too, she tells me. I don't know why she chose to phrase the question this way instead of using the safe but impersonal, "How are you?" The germination stage of friendship usually progresses with formalities, but since she chose an informal question, I felt invited to provide an informal answer:

"I started my period today."

Never in my life have I answered a question that way with a stranger who wasn't also a medical doctor. I've only met this woman once, but her response leaves me in awe.

"I knew it. I told my husband you were going to start your period today." She turns to her husband walking behind us who's chatting with Kallan about boats. "Honey, did you hear her? She started her period today!"

I stare, stunned: is this conversation happening? But I feel . . . seen, and not at all embarrassed to discuss my period with strangers on a street. I am intrigued that this wise woman has detected, with confidence, something so personal and intimate about me. "The moon," she says, pointing upward with a smile. "I knew it was your time." We find a sushi restaurant and the sake flows.

Sailing and world travel bring out parts of me that were hidden—perhaps suppressed—but either way, unknown to me. I grew up under traditional gender roles, so I understood femininity as prescribed duties rather than an energy—sensual, cyclical, flowing. The day I discovered my first period, I felt more shame and *hush-hush* than I did celebration of my joining the "menarchy." My body reflected that tension with irregular periods and bouts of cramping. My cycling felt like a rickety car trying to make it up a mountain: poorly resourced, and force-fed the wrong fuel. Doctors prescribed hormonal birth control. Never once did they say, "Try spending more time with the moon."

Now I request night shifts. With little to no exposure to artificial light, my periods sync with the lunar cycles, and I'm no longer afraid to release blood. Aggressive mood swings and cramping disappear. My energies turn cyclical too, with the middle of my months overflowing with spirited vitality, and the bookends of each month reserved for quieter, more internal meditation. With my moon-gifted rhythms, my mind loses its confused fog. I think back to days of reporting symptoms to my doctors. Their lack of acknowledgement of nature, her influence over human bodies, as well as the disapproval to delve into such realities, only amplified my soul problems. I could never find the words to explain such a malnourishment, but society's denial of such powers, rhythms, and seasons had worn on me to such a point where I no longer believed those spirits existed or cared about me. What a satisfaction to discover the moon hadn't forgotten me—wanted me; looked for me; found me.

Now I indulge in growing the key relationships in my life: pairing myself with nature and observing her influence over me. I know that nature has altered me physically. Like an owl, my eyes have developed a keen night vision. My skin picks up on shifts in windspeed. My ears detect sea animals and rain coming soon. My body craves more and healthier foods—depravity no longer serving me. My nose seeks to breathe clean, salted, or earthy air. I am barefoot. I am tanned, not burned, by the sun. I am aware now of what it is to be a living, breathing mammal on this planet.

Hi, Sheena.

It's nice to meet you.

Chronic soul problems: symptoms resolved.

***

"Bubbles!" she hoots, the pop of the Champagne bottle rousing her husband from his midafternoon nap in our boat's hammock.

"Yara, can a man sleep?" he asks, rubbing his eyes. He nearly falls out of the hammock. Yara, a dazzling and assured woman in her fifties moved to Bonaire from Brazil for a life restart. After raising her kids and signing her divorce papers, she focused her vision on vivacious living. Driven by an energy that appears with feeling done, complete, *finalizada*—with a marriage she worked hard at; with raising children she's proud of. Both were perfectly lovely experiences and now—life is about her. A svelte Brazilian chef named Paulo caught her eye one evening as she glanced up from her entrée, and that's when she saw it: what was to be the next chapter of her life. They fell excitedly in love, moved to Bonaire where they combined their resources and talents—Yara the sociable hostess and Paulo the talented chef—and opened a Brazilian restaurant a short distance from the sea. She prances toward him to lean on the hammock. He playfully swats her away.

"Wake up, sleepy! Bubbles!" She shimmies her sumptuous bosoms at his eye level, and it works: his eyes open wide. I pass her plastic cups, and bubbles are passed around.

We met Yara and Paulo through another sailing Brazilian couple we've befriended, Georgia and Diego. We all grew close while watching the World Cup over beer and dishes of açai yogurt—the yogurt because it was 10 a.m. when the game started, and the beer "because you can't watch the game properly without one," Yara had explained, splashing one down in front of me. One night over dinner (their treat) we mentioned moving onward to Curaçao. Yara threw her hands in the air and decided in an instant: "We need an adventure! We'll come with you and fly back! No problem."

Now we're all sailing to Curaçao. In exchange for their passage, they cook gourmet meals salted by the ocean and thrown over flames. Her husband has brought along *Picanha*—a cut of beef called a sirloin cap or "rump cover" in the United States. We grill outside while bubbles whet our appetites and loosen our spirits. Paulo's hair falls perfectly into his eyes as he times the meat's exposure to heat. Sweat drips down his cheeks and possibly falls onto our steaks but no one worries; it's hard to tell the difference between sweat and seawater when you're grilling in the middle of a wavy ocean. He's working on his English but depends heavily on Yara for translation. We're never quite sure if we're getting the exact translation, as she always interprets in a way that seems added to or subtracted from. "He says the meat will be ready soon." She adds a mischievous smile and wink, "and he says he has perfect meat." I love their love. It appears to be a love that doesn't require mental strategies to survive. What is it, then, that fuels their passionate commitment to each other? Their friendship turned romance unfolds before me. I relax back into my cushioned seat, rocked and misted by the waves to the soundtrack of Yara and Paulo's flirts and giggles. I look over to Kallan. That used to be us. He stands at the helm staring off.

The sun and breeze work together to warm and cool our freckled bodies. We drift into homeostasis in body and spirit. There's music and adjusting the sails. We try to beat our World Cup-watching friends, Georgia and Diego, who are sailing not far ahead of us. Georgia and Diego had agreed to transport the band members Yara and Paulo brought to the island from Brazil to play in their restaurant for the week. A trail of live music and jolly singing streams from the deck of their vessel.

We met Georgia and Diego on the sailing vessel *Unforgettable 3* in Bonaire. One afternoon, Kallan and I were returning from a dive perusing the reefs when we happened to pass their boat. I spotted them outside looking at footage on their camera.

"Stop!" I yelled over to Kallan, so he could hear my voice over the dinghy engine. "Young sailing couple! Let's be friends!" Kallan made a U-turn, and we headed over to their boat.

They waved, welcoming the interaction. You're never sure what language someone speaks when you pull up to a vessel, so Kallan started with "Ahoy!" and we become immediate and great friends. WhatsApp numbers were exchanged along with plans for meals and adventure outings together. Without knowing it yet, we were welcoming new friends with whom we'd sail side by side for the next six months.

The oddness of this—of calling over to complete strangers to offer friendship—won't dawn on me until I reflect on my journey after its end. Imagine choosing a random house in your town, knocking on the door, smiling, and saying, "Let's be friends!" And then having both parties commit to being active, lovely, consistent, *instant* friends. How quickly would the door slam in your face, if anyone even offered to open it for you? But here in the Caribbean, where the sailing tribe—the most independent of people—are deeply *inter*dependent, the impulse is natural and welcomed with enthusiasm. It's nearly expected. Sometimes you're the receiver of a friendly knock on your hull and sometimes you're the knocker. This giving and receiving is so invigorating for the human spirit. With every unexpected knock on our hull, I run outside with a childlike thrill to see who it could be.

Our time in Curaçao and Aruba is filled with open markets, scuba diving, yoga, and dancing on beaches over coconut-flavored drinks. Sand dots our feet, climbs up our legs, and makes its way into our kisses—kisses that are starting to feel forced, but I'm determined to kiss through the grit. I am stung by a jellyfish; little red knots rise in a line on my skin. We continue to watch Brazil kick their way through the 2018 FIFA World Cup to the quarterfinals with our new friends, clanking our beers and boasting, "*Mais uma*—one more!" after every goal they score. We host a party on our boat to watch *Captain Ron*, and we collect more friends, another young sailing couple: Ashley and Steve, with their Labrador retriever, Bella, on *Bella Vista.* Instead of a honeymoon, they saved to spend a year sailing together after their wedding. We spend our nights all gathered together—each night on a different host boat—in deep conversations of life, love, loss, and world politics while dunking tortilla chips in guacamole and plotting out our flotilla's crossing to South America.

These friendships reach beyond the surface. In sailing, female relationships are important and as strong as the double-braided lines reaching up our mast. It's through this female network that I find medical advice or assistance when needed, an empathetic ear, an extra this or that, food storage tips, birth control advice, a wine-night *amiga,* or relationship counselors. I meet women raising babies, mending clothes, suturing open wounds, running businesses, cleaning fish, exchanging books, scheduling barbecues, negotiating purchases, tracking budgets, *juris doctors* providing legal advice, and retired dermatologists giving skin cancer screenings, all while docking boats and pulling lines. They are as important to me in the sailing world as the integrity of the vessel I live on: they keep me afloat.

One evening during a boat party, I step outside to rinse a plate in the saltwater. Sitting on the last stair, I dunk the plate into the water and use my hand to brush it clean. My friends laugh in the background. I feel the moon wink at me.

CHAPTER TWELVE

Finding My Pace

"This passage won't be easy sailing." I overhear Kallan and Diego chatting. They sit in our galley looking at charts and plotting courses. I scoot in to review the charts. Due to the set-up of the land masses in relation to the water flow, we prepare for large swells and strong currents. We literally batten down the hatches—anything that could fall or find itself airborne we secure in a locked container, or strap in with a bungee cord. We provision in Aruba and place every bag of dry goods in places that will stay dry. We charge batteries on land and test our radios. When every boat and sailor feels ready—something I've become far better at—we set out for a crossing with our friends aboard *Unforgettable 3* and *Bella Vista.*

Radio reports come in: Pirates have been sighted off the coast of Venezuela. Fishing boats are stopping sailing vessels to ask for water and then greeting them with guns when they return with both hands full of the requested water. We leave a baseball bat near the door and hide our cash.

We hoist our mainsail. Our game plan is to stick close to our buddy boats, speak as little on the radio as possible, and keep a watchful eye out. We promise to check in with each other via our Garmin satellite communicators at each change of watch.

I'm on night watch. We've turned our navigation lights out. It's safer to sail here without calling attention to ourselves. Sailing without lights in complete blackness is the ultimate test in trust. We can only hope another vessel doesn't crash into us or that we don't run into something. Truth is we wouldn't know until we heard the loud bang or scrape announcing that it's too late to do anything anyway. We aren't the only moving objects out here without lights on—a fishing boat with a sleeping solo captain, a stray container that fell from a ship, a floating tree—anything can take you down if you hit it right.

I am reading my book with the help of a headlamp when I hear the radio crackle. "Ahoy, sailor . . ." a voice teases in a menacing way. The hair on my arms rises. I am paralyzed into stillness. I don't recognize the voice, and I know that our buddy boats are outside of radio range. We're only able to communicate through our satellite-based texting device.

"I see you . . ." the voice says, tauntingly. I jump from my seat, my book falling to the floor. I stare at the radio. "I seeeeee you." I run downstairs to wake Kallan. We are miles offshore, in international waters, nearing South America. It's two o'clock in the morning and we're surrounded by nothing but dark sky and darker sea.

I shake Kallan.

"Listen." The radio clicks.

"Where are you off to?"

He jumps out of bed and grabs the baseball bat. We close and lock the glass cabin doors. Then we sit, staring, facing the stern of *Seas Hope,* waiting. The waves push us onward. Time passes slowly. The only sound is that of the waves hitting the hulls.

We never figure out who played cat and mouse with us. When the sun rises, we step outside to look around, but there is nothing but miles of open ocean. At 9:47 a.m. we're off the coast of Venezuela, finishing off vegetable omelets. *Unforgettable 3* is sailing within a half-mile of our position. *Bella Vista* floats behind us.

Off our port beam, we spot an orange flotation device large enough to be a life raft. Kallan, still chewing his omelet, grabs the binoculars. "It's a life raft," he confirms.

"Is someone on it?" I ask, my eyes wide. He nudges his nose further into the binoculars straining to see.

"Looks like it," he says, throwing down the binoculars and running toward the radio.

Out this far, if you see a floating life raft, that means something *bad* has happened—like the sinking of a larger vessel has occurred or refugees are trying to leave one country to enter another—and who knows how long the occupants have been floating in the open sun and sea.

Keeping our eyes on the floating raft, we hail Georgia and Diego.

"We have what appears to be a life raft off our port side," Kallan reports. "We're going to check on it."

"I'll follow," Diego responds, turning his vessel around. In the nautical world, if you come across what *could be* a life raft, you must stop to offer help. You never know what or who you may find, but if you have a safe, operational vessel, the offer of help is required per the International Good Samaritan Law. Should you decide not to help, and this decision is discovered later, you are held liable and can be fined up to $1,000 and spend two years in prison. We reel in our fishing lines to keep them from tangling in our props and I lose sight of the life raft momentarily.

"Where is it? Where is it?" I repeat to myself, reeling in the line as fast as I can, bobbing up and down in six- to ten-foot seas. We are only twenty-three miles off Venezuela. *What if someone is in the life raft? What if they need medical help? What if they're refugees—what do we do, legally, in that case? What if they're dangerous or armed?* But we have to go. There is no not going. My morals—beyond the Good Samaritan Law—won't allow it. I couldn't possibly leave someone out here floating, sunburning, dehydrating, starving.

With the fishing lines in, Kallan changes our heading. Our bow turns to face the floating, neon orange raft that disappears on the downslope of every wave. I squint to keep focused on the float. At sea, it's easy to lose sight of anything small; everything is so vast and so similar. Kallan grabs my arm and points at a black crow standing on the side of the float.

"Do you see that crow? You may need to prepare yourself to see bodies."

I exhale through pursed lips. *Bodies. Lifeless bodies. Human, sun-roasted flesh.* I steel up and shift my eyes back onto the raft wondering if the rule book specifies what to do with a lifeless, sun-roasted human?

Once we're close enough to look over the edges, we see the raft is empty. *Thank God.* We gather the raft up and secure it on our bow in an effort to remove trash from the ocean and keep other vessels from experiencing the scare we just experienced.

We call Georgia and Diego to update them, and then point our boats back in the direction of Colombia.

Two waterway entrances lead into Cartagena, Colombia: Bocachica (Small Mouth) in the south, and Bocagrande (Big Mouth) in the North. We settle on a Bocachica approach, which ends up being a smart move because in 1778, Artonio de Arévalo constructed an underwater barrier at the Bocagrande entrance intended to sink vessels that might have piratical or warlike intentions from approaching Colombia. We enter alongside the tall ships, a parade of historical replicas representing different countries in Latin America. Their crews in starched white uniforms stand atop the rigging where the countries' flags fly proud. Families from all over cheer them along, and since we are following right behind them, we absorb the waves and cheers as we pass by.

"What an entrance!" Kallan dodges boats crossing this way and that in the busy harbor.

Once anchored in the harbor of Colombia, next to a giant U.S. Coast Guard ship, we hire an agent to secure our entry into Colombia, South America. We plan on doing some refitting and bottom work while we're here, and as American citizens, we are granted three months to stay. We show our passports, boat registration, leave a cash deposit to secure our stay, and then settle into the balmy one-hundred-degree temperatures of South America. *We actually made it to South America.* I let it sink in that the unexperienced sailor who left Norfolk, Virginia, thousands of nautical miles ago left as a scared, numbed, doubtful girl whose hands shook at the thought of mixing epoxy resin incorrectly. Now she's here, having helped repair a broken sailboat and sailed it to South America an awakened woman—unafraid to call herself a woman—unafraid of unknown shores, unpredictable waters, and unexplained outcomes. I smile when I think of how proud the alchemist would be of me. *That stupid book*, I laugh to myself, *it was right all along*. I close my eyes and let the smells and sounds of South America envelop me.

I am pouring coffee and pulling out my journal when, without warning, a powerful wind hits us. A "chicken ass," as they call it in Cartagena, occurs when the wind suddenly jumps from nothing to forty-plus knots. The wind comes barreling down the bay with nothing to stop it, and we find ourselves in a full-on, high-speed wind tunnel.

Kallan and I jump up, our coffee cups tumbling. The boat spins and jerks herself on the anchor chain in the exact opposite direction from where she had just been pointing. A sudden, powerful shift like that could yank the anchor from this muddy bottom. We're on full alert—watching, listening. Our anchor chain becomes tangled around the anchor. We are compromised. We no longer have sturdy holding. Our boat is dragging—fast—straight into a stone wall.

Kallan starts the engines. I shut the windows.

Kallan runs to the bow to start pulling the anchor up. I run to the helm to steer. I need to move *Seas Hope* toward the anchor Kallan's trying to lift. One of our engines is struggling; we are limited to 1500 RPMs on our port side. I compensate for this vulnerability and steer accordingly. Kallan pulls the anchor up as fast as he can. Mud is strewn everywhere.

Our boat with its weak engine is grabbed by the unstopping wind. During a chicken ass, the wind never stops to take a breath. It's a perpetual exhale that feels like a powerful, endless sneeze. I try to keep *Seas Hope* facing into the wind, but our forty-three-foot vessel presents a lot of resistance. Engine power is no match for chicken ass power.

We slide closer toward the wall. We're seconds away from collision.

At last, the anchor untangles. Having brought it all the way up, Kallan yells, "Push her as far as she'll go!" I hold my breath and push the throttles forward. *Don't give out! Don't give out! Seas Hope* lurches forward . . . and we're free. We steer out to sea to float around—away from stone walls—until the wind dies.

Kallan has told me many times in situations requiring our swift action: "Think clearly. Don't walk, but breathe." I find his choice of words fascinating. He never says "run" because running would be dangerous on a vessel, and running puts your brain and body in a state of panic. We always want to avoid amygdala hijack from compromising our ability to make sound judgments. Instead, he says, *don't walk,* which I always understand to mean "move swiftly but not so swiftly that you're compromised." The speed between "run" and "don't walk" leaves a lot of space to calculate what speed would be safe but effective for each unique circumstance as it arises.

The first time he said it to me was the first time our anchor dragged—something I didn't yet know was possible. Our boat, pushed by heavy wind, nearly slammed into a bridge jammed with 5:00 p.m. traffic. I didn't yet understand the physics of what was happening, and I didn't know how to help. In a state of powerlessness, I had a panic attack and couldn't stop crying. I couldn't breathe. I happened to look over and saw our sailing friends Suzie and Brad on the pier, waving their arms.

"Go pick them up!" I begged. We needed extra hands because I didn't know how to use mine yet. They were ready to offer theirs.

"Just sit here. Try to hold us pointing in this direction." I took the helm and Kallan dropped the dinghy in the water to scoop them up. Brad and Kallan tied the dinghy to the port side where our engine was down so we could use the dinghy's engine for power to steer *Seas Hope* to safety. All I had been able to do was sit there and panic.

That old impulse, bolstered by my flip-the-switch personality, was always to panic or run. I was either on or off; life was either just fine or catastrophic. With practice, I have gotten better at applying the think-clear-don't-walk-but-breathe principle on my own. In the Bahamas, we had to repeat the securing-our-dinghy-to-the-port-side exercise. This time, I piloted the dinghy as we took head-on waves exiting a cut of land to enter open ocean. I sat in the dinghy wearing a life vest with a small GPS locator attached to it (in case I went overboard) and hoped for the best. *Think clear. Don't walk, but breathe.* Waves crashed over me and into my face with force. The dinghy banged up against *Seas Hope*. I had to be careful to keep my fingers and hands away from the colliding vessels. Had my fingers been caught, they'd be badly broken and possibly torn off, and there is no easily accessible emergency medical help available in those isolated islands.

"Just a little farther," Kallan yelled, steering *Seas Hope* up and over the oncoming waves. A giant wave crashed over us and I fell to my side, my hand losing touch with the engine tiller. I pulled my body up and scrambled back to the tiller. When we finally got through, Kallan extended his arm, and I climbed up the side of *Seas Hope* to safety.

Living with nuance is a fluency I've learned. I trust myself here now. "Don't run" is less of a command and more of an invitation: I get to decide on the pace. I act quickly but not *too* fast. I am efficient. I am thoughtful. I trust my instincts. I trust myself. If I anticipate—waves, weather, circumstances, physics—I can figure out almost any situation and move with focused intention to a successful and safe end. Life happens with that nuance, and I feel confident, unthreatened, here, now.

***

Cartagena is the city of family, food, dancing, and enjoyment. Cartagena, in the summer months, is also the city of intense heat—it's nearly one hundred degrees by 7:00 a.m. In Cartagena, my vocabulary quadruples, and my Spanish speeds up thanks to a week in Spanish school and my need to make my way around the walled city. We take salsa lessons, and Kallan is bucked off an albino horse at a party miles inland, where we ate *sancocho*—meat, tubers, and vegetables served in broth—on a long wooden table in an open field in the countryside. One evening at a salsa club, a Colombian man twirls me with speed and precision around the dance floor, spinning me away from him and pulling me into him. My skirt tauntingly short. My bare feet feeling the pulse of the dance floor. I am wide-eyed and tipsy. He is sexy and sweaty. Kallan is ready to leave—the salsa club and Colombia. And though I fall deeply in love with South America, after the boat projects are done, it is time to move on. Our allotted three-month stay is nearly out of time.

Back at sea, our goal is to island hop through some of the twenty-seven different islets off the Cartagena coast—sparsely inhabited islands with white sand beaches and turquoise waters. It takes less than a day to hop between islands, but the few-hour sails keep us busy checking depths, charts, and winds.

We island hop:

Isla Baru

My windblown hair is pulled into tight braids by one of the island locals. We laugh and chat and share lemonade. These islands have no running water or power lines. Daily life for them, as for sailors, revolves around sunrises and sunsets. Coins are exchanged for papayas and freshly caught lobster, and we join a French couple aboard their vessel for dinner washed down with a glass of electric-blue Curaçao.

Rosario Islands—La Isla Grande

We anchor not far from Hacienda Napoles, the island party home of more than three hundred rooms that belonged to El Patrón, Pablo Escobar. We walk around the emptied out, decayed rooms of the world's infamous King of Cocaine. A small child waves to us from inside. Paint peels from stone. The pool is deserted. But when I close my eyes, I can feel the opulence there once was.

Isla Fuerte

Even before we've anchored at Isla Fuerte, we spot a kayak heading toward us. A young woman is waving. She slowly paddles around, waiting for us to get settled.

"I'm Laura," she says. She's a tattoo artist and graphic designer who lives part-time in Medellín and part-time on the island. Her father, an architect, is building an eco-friendly hotel for vacationers called "EcoHouse"—a hotel made of wood, topped with palm leaves, running on solar energy, and collecting rainwater. Laura walks all over the egg-shaped, roughly one-and-a-half-mile island introducing us to the locals (from among two thousand inhabitants)—people principally of African descent. We wave to a colony of sloths smiling upside-down in the trees.

This island offers mystery and magic. Henry Morgan, the renowned Welsh pirate, is rumored to have hidden treasures here in a cave. Ancient trees live here: the Walking Tree (a strangler fig) and La Bonga (a giant ceiba). I read that La Bonga's four-meter diameter trunk can be seen from space. Legend estimates it to be 2,500 years old.

"This tree knows so much, it cries," Laura says, pointing to what looks like a teardrop on her mighty trunk. I stand with the palm of my hand on her trunk and listen to her breathe as school children resting in her roots doze off for a late-afternoon nap.

When island hopping, we release any attachment we might have to a place; we dip in and out of life. No store on a visit is the same; no path we walk is familiar; there is no repetition in our daily experience. We're deep into overgrown jungles where the only way to find our way back is to strain our ears and hope we'll catch the sound of waves crashing on the shore, or babies crying, a sign of a nearby collection of homes.

My relationship with Kallan finds itself in a similar place: dipping in and out, overgrown, a fraying attachment, tears. I strain my ears hoping to hear something—anything—from him that will steer me back home to him. But just as the jungle hushes before a tremendous storm, all is silenced.

Sapzurro, Colombia

I white-knuckle a thick vine in my hands, a vine that oscillates between slimy and dried-out, its starting point deep within the jungle. From there it has grown unknown miles, twisting its way to reach the walking path for visitors to stumble upon. Standing on a ledge, I look ten feet down to the stream below at the leftover water trickling from a waterfall about a mile upstream.

"On the count of three, hold on tight and swing over to the other side," Kallan yells over, waving his arms to show me he is ready to catch me. My knee still throbs when I recall the last time I attempted this "Sheena of the Jungle" vine-swinging act—and ended up slamming my knee on an unsuspecting tree. I hobbled away from that experience, downplaying my pain so the rest of the travelers wouldn't be alarmed.

"I'm OK . . . I'm OK . . ." I had said through clenched teeth. But this time, I'm different. I'm bolder, I'm trusting. I'm ready. I tighten my fingers around the vine.

"One . . . two . . . three!" I engage my tummy muscles and gather my knees to my chest, the vine squeezed between my hands, arms, and legs. I fly over a stream full of rocks, past shoots of bamboo where monkeys judge my performance.

I am smiling.

The embodiment of freedom.

Then I am safe in Kallan's arms.

"See?" he says, letting me go. I had hoped he'd want to hold me a little longer. "No need to be scared." I wasn't scared: *Does he still see the old me?*

Leaving Colombia's islands and heading into Panama, we are run down by three Colombian military boats. Men pointing guns pull up next to our vessels.

"No nos dijiste que te ibas—You didn't tell us you were leaving," the man says, throwing one leg over our boat as he boards. I translate for Kallan and calmly show them our passports with our stamp approval "out" of Colombia. In Spanish, I tell them we are headed to Panama. "At any point, did you leave the vessel?" He asks, in Spanish.

"Nosotros caminamos en la selva—We walked in the jungle," I say.

"Did you check your boat when you returned?" Another man says, boarding our vessel. He repeats: "Did you check your boat when you returned?" Kallan shakes his head *no*.

"You need to check your boat. Drugs could have been planted on your boat without you knowing. Then they'll track it for pick-up in Panama when you leave your boat again."

We, along with the two military men, search the boat, opening hatches, lifting pillows, looking for anything that seems *off*. Everything appears to be untouched and in place.

"Viajes seguros—safe travels," he says, and they leave our boat. We see the other vessels are getting the same rundown. When we're all cleared, we carry on.

CHAPTER THIRTEEN

Decisions

We make it to Obladía, Panama, at the peak of rainy season, which lasts for seven to nine months annually. Within minutes, we collect forty gallons of fresh rainwater. Our five-gallon bucket is overflowing. Water spills over the edges and sloshes onto the deck. We're outside, clothes sticking to our skin, mopping down *Seas Hope* with fresh water from the sky, cleansing her of saltwater splashes. Gallons and gallons of rain fall. We have more than we need. Our tanks are full of fresh rainwater. Every jar, bowl, and dish we own is overflowing. Our windows leak. I make tea to put in the refrigerator. I shower outside. I do laundry. It rains on.

The name "Panama," given by the Cueva Indians means "a place where many fishes are taken." In October of 1852, standing where I am standing would have been a death sentence. These rains bring mosquitos—along with chikungunya, West Nile virus, Zika, malaria, dengue, and yellow fever, leaving grown men "withered as cut plants in the sun."[10] It was in 1852 that Ulysses S. Grant—while working on the Panama Railroad—wrote home: "The horrors of the road in the rainy season are beyond description." I see what he meant. Everything—but mosquitos—washes away, leaves you, slips into the ocean. A tidal wave of dirt transforms the blue waters to a stinky, thick brown goo that crawls. The fish swim away from the creeping, soupy earth from fear of being choked. Everyone—human, monkeys, reptiles, and even bugs—live in some state of wet.

We anchor in a cove surrounded by jungle that refuses to be tamed. The villages are hidden, but you can smell the fires. The

10. David McCullough, *The Path Between the Seas* (New York: Simon & Schuster, 1977)

monkeys holler, hoping for sailors' kids to toss an occasional Cheeto their way.

For some exercise and out of a powerful curiosity, we are drawn to enter the jungle with one machete and no map. The canopy of the jungle shields us and animals from the rain. Ants carry items five thousand times their body weight, weave a line off to somewhere. Twisted vines hang, tangled like electrical wires, thick, and hundreds of feet long—cables reaching from high in the sky down to the soaked ground floor, providing transportation and life for animals and jungle organisms on their journeys downward. Our machete is nothing against them. We can hear the jungle breathing, and we understand that the jungle hears us, too.

With his machete, Kallan carves our initials into the tough bark of a tree deep in the jungle: "K & S" with a heart around it. I'm surprised, a flash of our old giddiness for each other. Lately, it has been challenging to find space to be Kallan and Sheena—boyfriend and girlfriend. When we're sailing, we have our roles: Captain and First Mate. When we're out adventuring cities, islands, or jungles, we're tourists. But here, right here on this tree, a glimpse of the boyfriend and girlfriend.

"Let's go," Kallan says. I stand there staring at our initials a bit longer, then turn away.

Hours later, we push our way out of its lushness—out of the jungle, covered in mud. Splashes of water clean our shoes, legs, and hands and cool our faces. Refreshed, we return to our boat.

***

When sailors island hop, they usually spend a day or two at each island, depending on the availability of resources. On some islands we choose to leave without purchasing supplies or food because the islanders aren't going to have a delivery of supplies for a week or more, so we don't want to diminish their limited resources. Some islands are observing religious holidays and want to be left alone to celebrate. Out of respect, we move on. Some islands are without a single human soul. In these places, we sometimes anchor to sleep and enjoy a meal over open fire with our fellow boaters before continuing. Eventually, we pull the anchor and move on.

Puerto Escosés and Mulatupu, Panama (San Blas Islands)

We round the corner of a mountain full of lush, green jungle tangle. The charts of these waters are incomplete. What depths listed are vague or inaccurate. I compare our GPS to the chart. Plotting our true position on the chart suggests that our boat is fully on land. Our sails are out, harnessing eighteen knots of wind, pushing our vessel at a solid six-plus knots when suddenly . . . *grrrrrrrrrriiiiind!* Rocks grind against fiberglass. *Seas Hope* has hit a reef.

Kallan turns on the engines and throws them into reverse. We have to get her off of this fast. Otherwise, the waves will keep pushing her onto the reef, banging, banging, banging her to ruin. The grinding sound stops. She's clear.

Now we must quickly find anchorage so we can assess the damage. No time to worry about taking on water right now. I run to the bow. With zero assistance from the charts, I stand, assessing the depths visually. I've learned to read the water and how it reacts to underwater topography. I extend a guiding finger and Kallan follows. A thick cloud settles over us and drops buckets of rain. No time to grab my foul-weather gear. We have a potentially compromised vessel that needs to be anchored *now*. I stand against the rain searching for a safe anchorage. Soaked, barely able to see Kallan at the helm, I give him a thumbs up. He returns the signal and we drop anchor.

We notice a small group of fishermen hanging out on hammocks watching the downpour, their arms tucked behind their heads, feet crossed. Fish is cooking over a fire protected by their banana-leafed hut. These men, who know these reefs better than anyone, watch us struggle to guess what we couldn't possibly see or know. Safely anchored in thirty feet of water, I squint through the rain awaiting what's to come next. *Are we sinking?*

I can smell the fire charring the fish's flesh.

"I'm diving to check the bottom," Kallan says, grabbing his snorkel mask and jumping head-first into the water.

He resurfaces with the report. The bottom is fine: scratched, definitely hit, but showing no life-threatening puncture wounds. We grab towels and dab our dripping hair and soaked appendages. An invitation comes over the radio from our buddy boat, sailing vessel *Walkabout,* a husband-and-wife sailing duo from Sweden who joined us back in Cartagena.

"Irish coffee in thirty minutes?" Nils asks. He had seen us run aground—a little whiskey could help. We gladly accept, our skin chilled from the downpour.

Social interaction is good medicine when you're surrounded by waves, wind, and sea creatures—none of whom speak English. So, when Anneli and Nils of *Walkabout* invite us and another vessel in our traveling flotilla, Andy of *Wolfpack*, I'm down for a boat party. It's been more than fifteen days since I've had any contact with anyone outside of our travel group.

Travel groups are another form of guardian angel that appears in the sailing world. Every time you imagine yourself to be "out there" sailing alone, your imagination is usually wrong. Once, in the middle of the ocean when we thought we were completely alone, another small, private vessel came floating right by us, headed in a different direction. We all stood on the decks of our boats to wave to each other as we passed. And there always seems to be someone heading your way who's willing to make the journey with you—a reminder from the universe that you're never really alone if you're open to the delightful strangers willing to join you along the way.

We drop our dinghy and board our friends' boat. A piping hot cup of coffee abundant with rum and whiskey lands in my hands. Then silence. We see the local fishermen paddling over in their dugout canoe. I stand up and wave my friendliest wave. Before entering Panama, we had been told that the Guna natives are protective of their lands and waters.

"They're a fighting people," a Panamanian told us, while stamping our passport. "Be kind to their land, pay their tax, and don't overstay your welcome . . . if you *get* a welcome."

I learn later why they've been dubbed "a fighting people." They have fought wars against the Spanish and the Embera-Wounaan (another indigenous people living in Panama), and in 1925 they won in a revolt against the Republic of Panama.

An internet search yields stories of unhappy interactions between travelers and the Gunas of Guna Yala, some resulting in injuries. One year after our visit, a husband and wife with their two children will be awakened by a noisy sound of hooded intruders on the deck of their vessel in the middle of the night. The father is shot, and the mother is attacked with a machete, before the intruders run off with their fifteen-horsepower outboard engine. It's reported *much later* that the two suspects—identified only as "Panamanian"—were charged with aggravated homicide, robbery, criminal association, and mistreatment of a minor. It was also reported that the Guna helped track down the suspects, but when sailors are doing an internet search of places to anchor, these stories get blurry due to language barriers and unreliable reporting, so we end up banking on a post we read on a sailing forum: "Sailors don't typically have issues in the Guna Yala—but it's definitely possible." We hope for the best.

In 2010 there were 31,557 Gunas in Panama, none of whom call themselves "Guna." It's simply a name they allow *huaga* (foreigners) to call them. Most of them live among the forty-nine islands of San Blas in villages dependent on fishing, coconuts, and boaters passing through. Their village leaders, or *Sahilas,* make all the decisions.

All of this runs through my mind as I welcome the fishermen with a smile, though I don't know if they want to be welcomed or what their intentions may be. I catch myself, again, thinking of Columbus and the Taíno—they, too, did this similar dance of noticing each other and waiting to find out what happens next. We wait to find out. When they're closer, they wave back and hold up a basket full of coconut-smoked fish and neon green limes. We exhale a collective sigh of relief: it looks like we'll be getting a welcome instead of a fight. We humbly accept and they begin to board the boat, which makes Nils visibly nervous. Unsure what language they speak, I try Spanish first.

"Bienvenidos, amigos. Me llamo Sheena. Hablas Español?" They nod in confirmation. I find out they speak two languages—Spanish and Guna (or as they call their language, "Dulegaya," meaning "people-mouth.") The government of Panama—who delivers supplies and resources to the Guna every week or so—requires them to teach their children Spanish in their schools, but they speak Guna within their villages and families.

We pass them glasses of rum to show our gratitude for the fish and limes. They drink quickly. Our conversation begins slowly, mostly because my friends depend on me for translation and my Spanish is intermediate, at best. We start with basics: Their names are Jhon, Richard, and Lester. We are unsure if these are their real names or names they adopt when dealing with American travelers, but out of respect we call them the names they provide to us. We describe where we are from and what we are doing. We establish our ages and whether we have any children. The conversation stumbles into what foods are available in Puerto Escosés, but—interested in whatever goods we have—they suggest their village of Mulatupu instead. Jhon hands me a whole fish; he plops it straight into the palm of my hand.

"*Come tú—Eat!*" I look at the whole fish resting in my hand.

"*Con un poquito limón—with a little lime,*" Jhon advises, and he squeezes a splash of lime over my coconut-smoked fish. I grab a pinch with my fingers. The taste of white flesh and the zing of the lime (with the assistance of my Irish coffee) warms my body.

"*Refresco,*" Richard says, proud of his hard work to find, kill, prepare, and deliver this meal. Kallan and I want to present them with a gift to show our gratitude for their meal, and also initiate a relationship with Jhon, Lester, and Richard to ensure the safety of our own vessel.

"*Que necesitas? What do you need?*" I inquire.

"*Arroz? Rice?*" Lester asks, raising his eyebrows. Kallan returns to our boat then comes back with dried rice in a bag, a bottle of Hershey's chocolate, and canned milk. Their eyes light up and we say our goodnights.

When the sun rises the next day, we rub the sleep from our eyes to find our Guna friends sitting on our boat with a bowl overflowing with gigantic lobsters. We offer them café Colombiano and *chiclé.* With radiant smiles, they sip *café con azucar* and pop chewing-gum bubbles while we pull up the anchor. Our goal is to head to Mulatupu and, since the local Gunas know the deepest waters and most efficient way, Kallan turns the helm over to Richard, whose feet don't touch the floor when he's seated at the helm. Lester, the third of our Guna friends, places a necklace around my neck made from the teeth of a fish.

We tie their dugout canoes to the back of our boat. Jhon, Richard, and Lester are elated to take a ride on *Seas Hope.* They had paddled in their canoes from Mulatupu to procure food and other essentials for their families. They were to return with fish, coconuts, banana tree leaves (for the construction of their homes), and any game they could hunt along the way. Their dugouts now full, the paddle back to their families would have taken eight to ten hours. Aboard *Seas Hope,* they'll be home in less than one.

I read off the water depths—English for Kallan, Spanish for Richard, and we weave our way through, pulling the canoes behind. With their canoes full of findings being pulled faster than they're built for, they're tipping this way and that.

"One of them has to ride in the canoes while we tow them, to keep the boats balanced. Otherwise, they'll lose everything they've worked to collect," Kallan says. I translate the best I can, pointing to the canoes and miming the wobbling of their boats. In a dramatic display of arms, I show: "Everything will fall out." Lester gets it and hops into one of the canoes providing it more ballast.

We arrive in Mulatupu, still-full canoes in tow, and are invited ashore by our friends Lester, Richard, and Jhon to meet their families. While tying up our dinghy we watch a barracuda fly from the water and bounce along the surface hoping to catch the smaller fish attempting to get away from him—a Caribbean water-world form of cat and mouse.

The Guna people refer to themselves as *Dule* or *Tule*, meaning "people." Their village overflows with smiling faces. Babies bounce on hips. Children show off a trick with red strings. Lester's family welcomes us with smiles, and I pass out lollipops (*bonos* in Guna, also written as Kuna, a Chibchan language spoken by approximately fifty thousand people). His wife hands over a beautiful, hand-sewn *mola,* a handmade textile of maroons, oranges, yellows, and blues—traditional Guna women's clothing.

Jhon leads us onward to his family, along with a trail of small, whispering children. The Guna culture is a matriarchal society. The women own the land; the men move into homes where women are the leaders. His wife, Lula, welcomes us in and we sit in plastic chairs, resting on their concrete-floor home. A hammock hangs in the middle of the room. Family photos are nailed to the walls.

Lula disappears behind a hanging fabric and reappears to present me with another lovely blue, white, and red *mola.* We present her with gifts we stuffed in our bags on our way off boat: a packaged cookie, some hooks for hanging clothes or bags on, an entire box of gum, and a kitchen knife.

Jhon presents Kallan and me with a small live turtle that fits in the palm of my hand. I lift the turtle up to get a closer look.

Little beady eyes. Small feet. He's a lot like the beady-eyed, wooden turtle that hangs in our boat. I assume this is a family pet, so I express my awe and fascination and motion to hand it back.

"It's a gift for you," Jhon says, in Spanish. *"Hijo,"* he says, gesturing at Kallan and me.

"What does that mean?" Kallan asks.

"It means, 'son'...", I say, eyes wide. "He wants us to keep this." I look up. Jhon and Lula are smiling. Lula asks what we will name him, and in honor of their sweet family, Kallan says, "Jhon Guna."

Jhon's family laughs, and he takes me outside to pick hibiscus flowers to take home with us for Jhon Guna's dinner. The village children peek through the trees and giggle, watching our every move.

Toting the turtle in the palm of my right hand, we walk to Richard's family home. I feel his little nails scratching and his occasional retreat into his shell. We meet Richard's sweet wife and baby, who starts crying at the odd-looking visitors. They take us around their village, which includes a space for the mothers to birth children, a school (with internet connection available a few hours a day), two straw huts for congressional meetings, two bridges, and a few stores. The rest of the island is covered in bamboo or concrete homes with straw roofs. It's teeming with families, chickens, dogs, and pigs.

We are visiting five days before a political election. Signs hang everywhere, announcing that if you are at least seventeen years of age, you are expected to vote. Flags hang on each hut designating its occupants' preferred political party.

The sun fades. We wave our goodbyes and head back to the boat—anchored only eight hundred feet from their village—to boil pasta and partake of some of the lobster, crab, and snails the Guna presented us with.

Kallan and I are discussing our new baby turtle when we hear an *"Hola!"* from the stern of our boat. It's Jhon, Lula, and their fourteen-year-old daughter, Ina (meaning "medicine," something we find out she wants to study). We invite them aboard, happily splitting the pasta and sauce so there is some for all, accompanied by a glass of *agua fria*. It's Lula's birthday and they request that we sing "Happy Birthday" in English. Kallan and I oblige them, hands clapping.

As we clean up the plates, a serious tone falls on the evening. John and Lula exchange glances and Ina's eyes look hopeful. Jhon asks if we can take his daughter back to the United States with us. I am careful to note my body's reaction—*don't have one,* I tell myself. This wasn't an easy request for them to make and I certainly don't want them to read any kind of lackadaisical dismissal on my end. I point that I need to translate for Kallan who is washing dishes.

"Sí, sí," Jhon says, awaiting my translation. Kallan, hearing me, stops washing dishes and quietly scoots into the seat next me. I am thankful he hasn't left me to approach this on my own.

"He wants opportunities for her that Mulatupu can't provide," I say, listening to Jhon speak and translating. "She wants school and a career." When Jhon stops speaking, he awaits our response. Kallan reaches for my hand under the table knowing this won't be easy to explain.

I feel stopped in my tracks. I once asked the universe to provide me mentors, teachers, resources—specifically a way out of my fear of sailing. The universe provided me just that in the female sailors who took me under their wings without hesitation. The universe provided me a sisterhood in the form of my sailing teachers, in the form of guardian angels who helped me with a doctor when a doctor was needed. What if I am supposed to be her sisterhood? Her wings? What if she thinks I'm the answer the universe sent for her? How do I explain in English, much less basic Spanish, that politics will overpower all of this? I take a deep breath and slowly explain in the best Spanish I can muster. . . .

We are honored . . . but we cannot take his daughter.

Multiple hearts sink, mine included. I explain the process of how she could come to the United States: secure a Panamanian passport and then purchase a plane ticket and then . . . .

"But we have no money," Ina jumps in. The Guna trade mostly in products, time, or skills. Their potential to make actual money is limited to whenever a tourist happens by and whatever they're willing to pay for their handmade molas.

There's that feeling again.

I've observed this conflict many times as we travel south through the Caribbean. From an outsider's perspective, their subsistence lifestyle is romantic, peaceful, unhurried, and chemical-and-stress free. There are no health insurance hassles when you're being treated by the local medicine man or woman. There's no traffic or bureaucracy. How magical it is to receive nutrients straight from the sea with your own hands, to wear and fix clothes you make yourself, to birth and educate your own babies. But prosperity is relative. Isolation means lack of access to opportunities, and Ina's figured that out.

Ina speaks Spanish and Guna and she's teaching herself English. She has dreams beyond motherhood and mola-making. She sees the islands of her people drowning in waste—their own and waste from other countries that the ocean currents carry and dump on and around her homelands. But she doesn't know how to make change happen. She wouldn't have known any different, but when tourists started coming by with their fancy boats and different clothes, she began to wonder where they came from. Then, with an initiative funded by Panama, her school receives a few hours of internet each day: YouTube gives the younger generations of Guna clips of life elsewhere, and this has left Ina with a hunger her island can't satisfy.

I wonder if her desire to leave is a whimsical wish for something temporarily different. Here I am—a "wealthy American" in her eyes—looking at and loving her island, significant parts of me wishing for a life that passes in the ways she's familiar with. If she were to suddenly change places with someone in New York City as she wished, perhaps she'd be getting flipped off or dodging calls from creditors instead of enjoying a meal fresh from the sea with her family.

I run downstairs and grab a book, a notebook for writing, and a set of oil paints and brushes. I sit next to her.

"This is a book in English. It will help you learn vocabulary and sentence structure," I say, pointing out specific chapters. "This is a notebook for writing." I flip the pages revealing blank, open space for her thoughts and learnings.

"*Para qué? For what?*" she asks.

"Para escribir lo que piensas. To write what you think," I respond. She flips through the empty pages. "Paint and brushes," I say. Her eyes open wide. "*Para pintar tu mundo como sueñas que sea. To paint your world as you dream it to be.*"

"*Y un día vive ese mundo—and one day live that world*," she says. I smile and nod my head, yes, yes, yes. Inside her gifts, I tuck one of my cards that includes my e-mail address and phone number. I want to be her sisterhood, and I hope to hear from her again.

Linton, Colón, Panama

We spend over a month deep in the islands of San Blas, swimming in clear waters, chasing thunderstorms, drinking beer, perusing molas, attending barbecues thrown by fellow cruisers, stunned speechless by sunrises and sunsets. I haven't seen a single car, street, grocery store, or vegetable, much less Wi-Fi or cellular service, in nearly two months. I am learning what I can live without, and that comes with a lightness I haven't felt before. Life boiled down to the physiological needs: air, water, food, shelter, sleep, and clothing optional.

We get to know the villages and learn their ways. When one of our buddy boats inquires about buying a bottle of rum, a young boy runs off to seek the approval of their chief. Since the villages only get deliveries every so often, whoever walks off with their rum must be approved by the chief, who must decide whether physical American cash is more or less important than the bottle of rum in an economy that doesn't trade in that.

When our sailing convoy arrives at a marina in Lintón Bay, we resurface after visiting a different time and place. We feel relaxed and refreshed, but as we drop anchor, a neighboring catamaran advises us, "Lock your doors at night; there's been a flurry of robberies lately."

From our anchorage, we can see a small gas station that sits at the edge of a jungle. Having run out of chocolate and beer and needing to check in with our families after months of silence, we head in. We lock our dinghy to the *muelle* (dock) and walk over to the building. Monkeys dangle from the trees awaiting treats dropped or forgotten by humans. People with sun-blistered, leathery skin sit smoking cigarettes and chasing the smoke with swigs of cheap beer. It is 11:00 a.m.—happy hour for the regulars here.

"New ones," a tired woman says in a scratchy voice as we approach. She flicks her cigarette ash and a little stray dog runs to lick it up. "Come on in and hook yourself to the life support machine," she says motioning to the struggling Wi-Fi router. She sings this as if she's a nomadic worker of a traveling carnival inviting us to *Step right up! Everyone leaves a winner!* Her pink shorts are too large—

or maybe she's become too small—and her hair is yanked into a messy ponytail running down her sweaty back. A steady beeping of unknown origin—I don't think it could be the router—does sound like a heart monitor, so I get her joke. Everyone has their heads bowed, staring at their screens. Only two electrical outlets are available, and both are taken. *Shit, the solar panels only got me to twenty-eight percent. Ah well, it'll have to do.* I grab a chair, type in the Wi-Fi password taped to the plastic picnic table, and wait for it to connect.

Missed downloads:

465 emails—*none of importance.*

200+ Facebook notifications—*none of importance.*

200+ Instagram hearts and sixteen comments—*none of importance.*

I had missed nothing.

I look over toward the woman with the sing-song voice and the big shorts. She's staring at me dead-eyed, sucking on her cigarette, her fingertips dyed brown from tobacco. She swivels her right leg, fidgety, bored.

"Twenty years ago, you would have never seen this," she says, waving her hand toward the group of travelers, all logged in. She's speaking to no one specifically. The constant beeping continues as conversations are held over it in Spanish, Dutch, Portuguese, German, and English—discussions of canal travel, hurricanes, one-night stands, brushes with the police, and "the good ol' days."

"The devices capture everyone's attention these days, but if I was a bombshell blonde strutting my stuff through here, oh, you'd notice," the woman says, rolling down the waist of her too-big shorts.

I get the impression this woman has been here for a while, decades possibly. And she's probably done her fair share of strutting. She misses it; I can understand that. Everyone knows her name; some avoid her. Perhaps she came here to catch a ride through the canal and just never caught the ride. I've seen many versions of this woman—barnacles who get stuck somewhere and survive off nicotine and cheap *cerveza.*

My mind drifts to a character from the book I'm reading, a real-life woman of Panama's past: Marie Doughty met her future husband in Texas in late 1882. Overcome with yellow fever, they were both nearly dead. A grave had already been dug for Miss Doughty, but she and her future husband, Dr. William Crawford Gorgas, survived. This rendered them immune to the illness, and they were married. Dr. Gorgas would later be assigned to serve as a U.S. Army surgeon during the building of the Panama Canal. He was to be the only official who followed through with his work—that is to say he *remained alive* and did not resign from the canal project.

One Panama night, not unlike the one I'm experiencing right now, Miss Doughty wrote in her journal while watching her husband smoke a cigar: "There is an alluring something about a night in the tropics." She imagined the ghosts of the past—the people who had come before she and her husband arrived to conquer the massive project of constructing a canal while also trying to survive. Here I am, 114 years later, experiencing an alluring tropical night in Panama, trying to survive, imagining her. People imagining ghosts imagining ghosts.

As I sit slapping mosquitoes, I am thankful for Dr. Gorgas and his small team's medical discoveries during the start of the eighteenth century. His work uncovered what we know today of Stegomyia fasciata (the mosquito that carries the yellow fever parasite) and Anopheles (the mosquito that carries the malaria parasite). Both of these mosquitoes are present in my daily life. But because of his work, we know to remove standing water on our boat, to use screens on our open windows, and to cover our sleeping bodies with a sheet, regardless of how hot we may be.

Kallan and I didn't get any Caribbean-specific vaccines before leaving America. I didn't even think to ask a doctor if any were recommended. I found out later that when traveling to the Caribbean, doctors suggest getting vaccines for hepatitis A, typhoid, malaria, yellow fever, and cholera, along with potential boosters of the vaccines given in childhood: measles/mumps/rubella (MMR), tetanus, diphtheria and pertussis (Tdap), chicken pox, polio, and influenza. Armed with only our childhood vaccines, we followed Gorgas's mosquito sanitation methods and, again, hoped for the best. Fortunately, we don't fall prey to mosquito-borne disease.

I bring my focus back to my computer. Kallan and I want to transit the Panama Canal—it's a bucket list experience for sailors. To do so is expensive—around $3,000 for vessels less than sixty-five feet; $5,000 to $10,000 for container ships—but there are "free" ways to experience this man-made magnificence: we can work as linehandlers (or crew) for a vessel planning to transit the canal. For a vessel to safely transit the canal, four linehandlers are required: two for the bow, two for the stern. An agent can secure them for a boat captain, but that'll cost $100 per person, and they often have little knowledge of sailboats and/or only speak Spanish. This is where people like Kallan and I come in—people, and there are many of us, who are familiar with sailing vessels, speak English, and who want to experience the Panama Canal's brilliant water lock system, but don't want to take our own vessel through it. So, I post an ad:

"Two knowledgeable, English-speaking linehandlers available ASAP, looking to experience the Panama Canal." I include a photo of us and my e-mail, then snap my laptop shut.

We head back to *Seas Hope* and sit outside on the bow, taking in the sights and sounds. The moon rises gracefully into the sky, and I feel interweaving connections: Dr. Gorgas and Marie, the hum of the locks opening and closing, our own families back home with their day-to-day struggles, and right here—Kallan's and my unspoken struggles. I feel the world around me, interconnected, locking and then opening; an inhale giving in to an exhale.

I know the moon sees it, feels it all, too.

I open the pantry and peruse our selection of stores: spaghetti, quinoa, couscous, amaranth. After a long time without access to a store, we have no sauces, not even olive oil or butter. We picked up our regular haul from the vegetable truck this morning—*lechuga, tomates, ajo, cebollas*—but we are down to bare bones.

"I'm hungry," I say, pulling my hair into a ponytail. There's a bus leaving at noon to Portobelo. For $1.50 each, we can secure a bus ticket, find a store, and stock up on our favorite sauces, cereals, milk, bread, and eggs. Also, our turtle needs fresh hibiscus flowers. We pack a backpack full of canvas grocery bags and run to catch the bus. We're on the side of the road snipping hibiscus flowers when a rusty rectangle of bright oranges and reds rolls up like a flame tearing through the green and wet jungle.

"Bus is here," Kallan says, laughing at the bus décor.

A red boa of feathers outlines the rearview mirror. Music is blasting. This old school bus was shipped here from the United States after it was deemed to be no longer safe there. The leather seats are slashed open, exposing the moldy cushioned innards. The windows are scratched, shattered, or nonexistent. The bus appears to be held together with red tape. The brakes squeal as it stops to pick up even more people. Parents smack the backs of their children's heads, wives lecture their husbands, and the bus driver just took a sip of something from a flask.

The bus speeds toward Colón, slowing only to take on large hills—with pops, strains, and sounds of mechanical distress. "If the bus starts rolling back, let's hope the brakes work," Kallan says, laughing.

Neither of us is sure when to get off the bus, so we wait for what feels right. I scoot in next to him and find a comfy place under his arm. We soak in the cuddles, stealing some kisses, and laugh at each bump of the road that threatens to untangle us.

"Here," I decide, randomly, with zero evidence of a grocery store. "Let's go see!" We pass the driver our $3.00 and hop off the bus.

"Hey, you want weed?" the driver asks. "Jorge gives you free popsicle when you buy from him." Tempting. I do love a popsicle in tropical heat. We wave to the driver—and turn around just in time to see a cab driver slam into a street dog. The dog hobbles off, holding his hurt leg high in the air. Locals run after him, collect his hurting body, and carry him to the local veterinarian as the Catholic Church opens its doors and people pour out. Some look refreshed; others wipe tears from their eyes.

We restock on supplies, tossing glass jars and boxes of pastas into canvas bags. I've been wondering: Should we get married? We've been dating for nearly three years and most of that time has been on *Seas Hope* where we've accomplished impressive couples sailing. Every time we're invited to another boat for a party, they tell us: "One year of being together on a boat equals forty years of marriage." By that math, we've been married for nearly eighty years and, mostly, we've been good. Maybe that's why I've felt some distance between us. Maybe he's, once again, waiting for me to be ready to jump in with both feet, then everything will lighten up after we *really commit*. We have considerably more moments of laughter than disagreements. *Right?* My phone is full of picture-perfect couple selfies. As challenging as fixing up an old boat and sailing her thousands of nautical miles has been, we still love a good make-out session and find each other irresistibly attractive. *Right?*

"Should we get married?" I ask, standing in the bread aisle. Kallan slowly turns to look at me and puts a can of green beans back on the shelf.

"Is that what you want?" he asks, placing his hands around the outside of both of my arms and looking me in the eyes. "I don't really see myself with anyone else, so if it's what you want . . . ."

Back in the Bahamas, Kallan had awakened me one morning with coffee ready, his fingers brushing through my hair. The sun and breeze managed the boat's temperature beautifully. I slowly opened my eyes to find him smiling and watching me sleep. Without a word, he handed me the coffee cup and a box.

"What's this?" I'd said, sitting up in bed and stealing a sip of the hot coffee, the box resting in the palm of my free hand. I set my coffee down and cracked open the box, peering inside. It was a diamond—his grandmother's—glimmering, proportionately cut, colorless. It sat in the box free, without a setting. At that moment it caught a beam of tropical sun and came alive. I looked at him with sand dollar eyes.

"I want this to be yours one day. I asked my mom to bring it to me before we left."

"It's stunning . . ."

"One day we'll get married, and it'll be yours."

Since then, we'd been waiting for some kind of . . . certainty. A sign? Maybe just waiting to breathe after the chaos of preparing the boat to see if our relationship had any sea legs of its own? Standing in the Panamanian market, we aren't sure if it's necessarily *right* to get married, but it doesn't feel wrong. It's something we certainly *could* do and if we gauge a future marriage off of our experiences thus far, we know there will be adventure, lovemaking, bold living, and the occasional disagreement that we seem fairly good at working through *while sailing a forty-three-foot boat.*

"It could be fun, I think." *Right?*

We land a linehandling gig on a boat named *Hogfish Maximus.* Kallan and I are selected along with a Russian artist traveling the world because she believes you only get a one-way ticket to life and a local Panamanian wanting to learn English. The Panama Canal is busy, so when they can send multiple small vessels through together at the same time, they will. *Hogfish Maximus* ties up to our friends on *Walkabout.* They call this center-chamber lockage, where the boats are rafted up two or three abreast. In fact, yachts can also moor alongside a tugboat or small tourist cruise ship. Our transit is scheduled for evening, meaning we're going through these colossal locks in the dark of night. In front of us: a cargo ship.

We enter the canal from the Atlantic side. Geographically, the Atlantic and Pacific oceans are not at the same sea level—the Pacific sits about twenty centimeters higher than the Atlantic due to less dense water as a result of the prevailing weather. We are about to experience some of the greatest engineering ever undertaken—humans lifting then lowering vessels over a land mass in order to connect two differently leveled seas. The Panama water lock system will raise our attached vessels eighty-five feet above sea level, then we'll rest for the remainder of the night in the manmade Gatún Lake to wait for the descending locks to reopen the next morning. Each chamber is 1,000 feet by 112 feet. The vessels are so tightly packed inside each lock there is seemingly no room on either side.

The locks, their electric motors, as well as the flooding and emptying, are managed from a control tower. The cargo ship in front of us enters the lock and is controlled by electric towing locomotives, which are on cog tracks along the lock walls. A fender chain is stretched between the lock walls because, should the cargo ship be moving too rapidly—heading toward damaging the historic doors—the chain will bring the vessel to a stop. Since our vessels are far smaller than the cargo ship in front of us, we don't need the electric towing machines; we have humans—canal employees—holding the other side of the line I'm holding and walking along the lock walls to maneuver our vessels.

Once everyone is settled in, the control tower begins the process. Gravity pulls water in from Gatún, Alajuela, and Miraflores lakes, which are fed by the Chagrés River. Water is rising and fast. The linehandlers on land are pulling in line as we rise, and I keep the line taut on my end. We ascend through the three different locks, which ultimately raises the vessel eighty-five feet from sea level to reach the level of Gatún Lake. I am mesmerized. The spotlights; the mighty steel doors; the deep hum of the locks opening and closing; 26,700 thousand U.S. gallons of water rushing in to fill each chamber—we float toward the sky. We complete three locks and settle in for the night in Gatún Lake, which serves as the water supply to operate the locks system of the Panama Canal.

It's a cloudy morning on *Hogfish Maximus* when Kallan wakes me up, takes me to the front of the vessel, drops to one knee, and proposes where the two oceans meet—proposes that we "keep the adventure going." *Had I pressured him? Shit, I pressured him.* He slides a temporary, stand-in ring onto my finger, a ring we purchased together at a market in Charleston, South Carolina, a ring that has been snorkeling and pulling lines with me ever since. *He doesn't look sure; he doesn't look . . . excited.* I manufacture tears—*maybe I'm not excited either.* Onlookers clap and cheer. My body is taken over, I'm performing all of the gestures I had seen from others' happy engagements: hands covering my mouth; the look of shocked delight; the delicate removal of tears; then cupping of his face as he tries to get this over with. Then the hug and the tears and the. . . .

"Yes."

Suddenly, we are fiancés. We look at each other—but don't say a word—did we mean to really just do that? *It could be fun.* I think.

It's not lost on me that I find myself on a lake between the world's two deepest oceans while I'm also standing in the middle of deep uncertainty, again. Maybe this isn't right for us. Maybe we could make it work. Then the real thought pushes its way through: maybe this isn't right . . . *for me.*

No time to figure it out right now. We have to make our way through the descending locks, from the Atlantic to the Pacific. Internal tensions within each of us strain Kallan's and my interactions with each other. *This should feel happier. Right?* We book a hotel room in Panama City for $30, where we meet up with our friends Georgia and Diego, who are already there provisioning. The hotel room feels palatial compared to the small deck of a monohull. I marvel at the lavish supply of hot, hot water pouring onto my sunscreen-covered limbs. The stillness of the bed shocks my system: I've lost my confidence with my *land* legs. We turn off the air conditioning, our bodies incapable of tolerating the manufactured freeze. I pull on a dress for Champagne and celebration.

Fiancés! I have never been such a thing. I don't think I realized there was so much performance to it all—*or maybe it's not like this for everyone else*. I believed on that cloudy day on *Hogfish Maximus* that our hearts would come together—that we could marry and develop an interesting life together. But if I had been ready to be honest with myself, I would have seen that the gray clouds hanging over us that day were signs of more than oncoming rain. Something was on the horizon for us. I knew it that day, and so did he. We didn't feel the elation we were supposed to feel after the proposal. Kallan even said, "Ehh . . . it's okay. It's not a big deal," when the first mate of *Hogfish Maximus* said, "We need Champagne!" But neither of us were strong enough to discuss the secret dread that had crept up and squeezed off our throats, silencing our voices now that my Charleston ring had switched from my right hand to my left.

"COUPLE CHOKES ON OVERSIZED COMMITMENT"

We're silent during the elevator ride down to the first floor where we're meeting to celebrate with the surrounding canal-transiting boats. We aren't sure why, but silence definitely feels better. As soon as the doors open, the performance begins. "The happy couple!"

"Oh, just look at you!"

"Congratulations!"

"Do you know what kind of dress you want?"

"You caught a good one!" The guys close in on him, and we're separated.

We dance under the moonlight on the streets of Panama City. The other couples dancing next to us sending us the occasional wink. I glance at the moon. She seems to say: *It's OK to not know what you're not meant to know yet.* I pass time the way I pass nautical miles—by allowing each moment to move me forward as it comes. The dread I feel is similar to the dread I felt the day I left on this journey—and look at how much I've loved sailing. *It'll grow on you,* I tell myself. I keep dancing.

Later, we call our families. We make a formal announcement and celebrations start in various places around the world. Except within us. We fall into the hotel bed on opposite ends and fall asleep facing opposite directions.

Think clear. Don't walk, but breathe.

The next morning, we taxi back to the Atlantic side of Panama to continue life aboard *Seas Hope*. We're in the back seat of a truck with supplies in the truck bed, and every time we stop, the driver tells us to keep our eyes on our supplies because locals are known to grab bags out of the back.

In Panama City we heard stories of the magic of the Chagrés River, so we've added that to our "next destination" list. Most of our stops have been planned based upon the suggestions or stories of sailors traveling the opposite way.

The truck pulls up to our marina and the driver helps us off-load our supplies, which have safely made the return home. Monies exchanged, we quietly grab numerous bags each and walk—both of us, weighted down—to the dock where we left our dinghy. We lift anchor and we don't say it but we're both thinking the same thing: getting back to our "normal" will be good for us. What just happened—our engagement—is still settling. How surprising to discover that what just happened feels like mold growing in our stomachs.

Chagrés River, Panama

The Rio Chagrés is very much alive.

Birds fight and celebrate.

Bugs work.

Jaguars breathe.

Herds of wild pigs rove.

Water slaps.

Leaves fall.

Wood cracks.

I am overwhelmed with the landscape and my eyes stay open wide.

Waterfalls cascade.

Branches pop, weighed down by the feet and hands of monkeys swinging. The leaves forecast the weather. Observe closely enough, and you'll hear a storm's approach minutes before the water begins to fall. Steam rises from ancient, lightning-struck trees.

Kallan wraps his arms around me from behind and kisses my neck. I smile. *The melt of tension I've been waiting on.*

This river also needs love and understanding. Between 1870 and 1914, the French and the Americans charged with engineering the canal feared the Chagrés. Historical records list the river as "the enemy" to canal construction objectives. The river, that once carried pirates Francis Drake and Henry Morgan through the jungle, is most dangerous in November—the month Kallan and I are here. I imagine people long before me also paddling down this river, smiling at the same calls from the birds, startled by the demanding hollers of the monkeys. I imagine the Americans cursing this river when the Chagrés floods swallowed their railroad and Gamboa Bridge. The Chagrés is wild, feral, unforgiving. Born during volcanic eruptions, she's witnessed massive land shifts, migrations, colonies of the Chinese, Hindustanis, and Malaysians, greedy and vengeful pirates and even watched as Christopher Columbus stepped off his boat in 1502, his last and final voyage. She has no agenda to support manmade plans or schedules. One doesn't label the Chagrés "the enemy" without repercussions. I want to show the Chagrés something different than unappreciative force. She, like everyone, only wants love and to be free to exist in her innate power. I was once her. I open my heart to her. I let in her wild, her resilience, her desire and devotion to exist. I whisper, "I see you. I hear you. You're impeccable—faultless."

We motor in our dinghy through the divergent cutouts created by French engineers in their effort to control the floods of the Chagrés during the rainy season. The water changes color based on where you travel, shifting from deep teal to navy to mocha brown and to raw, *sangre* red. I spot a small waterfall and we tie off the dinghy to a nearby tree to climb up in search of its source. We push through branches—gently, respectfully—following the sound and flow of water. The sound gets louder: she wants us to be here. We find a shower-like waterfall, cascading waters, pooling, cradled by rock. The lushness of the trees and tropical leaves keeps us hidden from the outside world. This deep inside the jungle, there are no human eyes to be shielded from, and the monkeys don't care. We slip off our clothes and step into the chilled rainwater tumbling from the mountains, surrounded by fragrant tropical flowers.

I tilt my head back and let the water run over my face. Kallan runs his fingers through my hair and rests his forehead on mine. *Why aren't our bodies coming alive for each other anymore?* He kisses my neck. *This is the man I'm marrying. Come alive, body. Come alive.* The jungle leaves us be, but my mind doesn't. *What's missing here?*

Back at the boat that night, after Kallan falls asleep, I take my journal outside to sit with the moon. She's splashed across the trees hanging over the Chagrés; both seem to already know what I'm just now realizing. They're waiting for me to say it. There's that voice again; I glance at the moon: "You're ready. You can say it." I grab my pen and I write: "What's missing?—*Nothing at all.* Instead, something new is here: a new me. I love her more than I love life with him."

***

We awake to Thanksgiving Day: We host our friend Andy, of *Wolfpack*. We'd met him in Colombia, where he sailed from Florida in a Halman 20 with one random crew member he'd picked up in Curaçao—someone just looking to hitch a ride to South America. *Wolfpack* is an old Canadian build of a European design called the Nordica and is generally known for coastal sailing. Sailing experts recommend vessels between thirty-five and forty-five feet when crossing oceans, so when Andy showed up on a *twenty-footer* claiming to have made his way here from *Florida*, everyone stared, impressed. An average-sized human can't even stand up straight in the hold. Throughout his voyage to Colombia, Andy told us later, he'd suffered hallucinations from sleep deprivation, and when the waves got frighteningly large for his small vessel, he'd grabbed his ditch bag, fully planning on being thrown overboard, fearing for his life. But he somehow arrived safely in Cartagena, beard stubble and cigarettes in tow, where he befriended Kallan and me. His crew member disappeared into the people of Colombia, and Andy climbed aboard *Seas Hope,* introduced himself as a friend who intended to stay. Since then, he's sailed alongside us for months as we've explored the islands of Colombia, San Blas, the Panama Canal and now the Chagrés River. He snapped photos of us when Kallan proposed even though he claimed to have sworn off love a long time ago. "Don't believe in it," he'd say, popping a cigarette between his lips.

I am pouring glasses of wine for Andy, Kallan, and myself when the Chagrés changes her mood. A little history: Engineers of the canal dammed this beautiful river, twice. They dropped large stones in her, then filled the spaces between the stones with thick mud until, eventually, she was controlled. In fact, the entire plan of the Panama Canal depended on whether or not they could use the Chagrés. Eventually, they pull off this earthen dam, constructed in 1913. Constructed by Lieutenant Colonel George Washington Goethals, the Gatún Dam does two things: first, it controls the everchanging water levels and speed of the Chagrés and the Gatún Lake from flooding the locks. Too much rain too fast can flood the locks and the land around them. Secondly, damming her resulted in the creation of the artificial Gatún Lake. When one hundred inches of rain falls in the rainy season, everything overflows, so the spillway opens up, and water rushes from Gatún Lake into the Chagrés. The canal, then, depends on the Chagrés to be the supplier of the 183 million cubic feet of water needed to fill Gatún Lake, as well as the receiver of overflow waters. This means when the fourteen gates supported by concrete piers open on the dam, pent-up water rushes with a fury from the manmade Gatún Lake. The only warning that those doors are opening are a few blares of an alarm. You don't want to be swimming at that moment—you'd be swept away.

We turn our attention to the anchor and wait for the waters to calm. The water slows. A hush settles among us. So much of sailing—life—is riding the fluctuations of concentrated chaos and then resettling into calm. One minute you're hyperaware, and the next you're wondering if you're floating out here forgotten. We clink our wine glasses and celebrate the many moments we find ourselves thankful for. In true form, I open my journal to make a list.

I'm thankful for:

- the jobs I lost and the free time I gained.
- the boat that taught me to believe in rehabilitation.

- the universe who has, to my surprise, provided me everything I've asked for and imagined.
- the fear I gave up and the courage I now hold.
- the naiveté I've discharged and the wisdom I've acquired.
- the past wounds I'm finally able to see.
- the antidote of nature.
- the partner who stands by me pulling lines, clinking glasses, fileting fish, and loving me.
- the nautical miles that taught me staying power—there's nothing to do but wait.
- the friends who are my arsenal of support and joy.
- the sea animals who stay with me as we float alone "out there."
- the birds who signal to me that land will soon appear.
- the vined plants protecting me as I swing across streams.
- the moon who shares with me her wisdom.

We spend the evening basking in our thankfulness, watching the sun put herself to sleep, and listening as the Chagrés gives and receives.

***

The next morning, we stand on a black sand beach at the mouth of the Chagrés, looking for sea beans. I first heard about sea beans when a woman with frazzled red hair and a scar on her left cheek held up her jar of the treasures in the Bahamas. "Sea beans. Once you find one, you'll be addicted to finding more." She had 372 of them resting in her sealed jar.

Sea beans—also known as "sea hearts"—are called *fava de Colón* or the "Columbus bean." Stories say these sea hearts inspired Christopher Columbus to travel west in search of new land. When he found them washed ashore, he knew they were not native to the Azores. Carried by the sea, they *had* to have come from somewhere else and he was determined to find out where. These beans developed a reputation as good omens for sailors, who were incentivized to find them because of this logic, as Stan Ulanski puts it in his book *The Gulf Stream*: "If they can stay adrift a year or longer to reach European shores, they can protect their owners on their long and perilous journeys."[11]

For twelve months now I've kept an eye out for these mysterious, protective, and lucky sea beans, but I have yet to find one. Previously, my irritation at not finding one would devour me. Eat me alive—whole days ruined. I remember the woman saying, "You don't find sea beans. Sea beans find you. When they feel you're ready, they will suddenly and without explanation . . . *be seen*."

I walk along the beach taking in the sounds and feels around me. I pick up a piece of driftwood and scoot sea debris aside. I close my eyes and inhale deeply. There's salty water, wind moving my hair, and I feel my weight sinking into the black, glittering sand. All is peaceful outside of me, within me. I slowly open my eyes.

There it is! A sea bean, perfectly round and smooth, untouched by any of the sea debris; not a grain of sand has scratched its surface. I flip it over in my fingers.

"I'm so glad to see you," I whisper to the sea bean before finding my voice and yelling, "Sea bean!" Kallan runs over to see. I hold the sea bean in the palm of my hand.

"Good eyes!" My eyes have changed a lot over the course of our journey together. Where I once saw only fear, competition, jealousy, shame, injustice, and anger, I now see patience, the pace of nature, the trust of the universe, and the magic of not needing to know—or possess control of—anything. Mostly, now I see me. There she is. A woman I adore and believe in.

---

11. Stan Ulanski, The Gulf Stream (North Carolina: University of North Carolina Press, 2008).

CHAPTER FOURTEEN

Unravel

Reggae music greets us as we pull up and anchor next to a bumpin' hostel. Drunken guests jumping into the water and hanging off inner tubes wave to us as we float past. The vibes aboard *Seas Hope* are strained with good intentions. I want our relationship to work. I am endlessly thankful for this adventurous life we're living together, but I'm realizing that may be where those feelings end. Maybe I came out here thinking I'd find a husband, but instead I found myself. I think he wants our relationship to work, too. He cares for me, and when he needed a first mate to believe in the journey and leave with him, I followed—but that, he's realizing, may be where his feelings end. Still, we haven't found the strength to voice these truths, so we try for each other. On our voyage to Bocas del Toro, we start dreaming up and writing down plans for our future wedding. We start with a date.

"Do we have to set a date right now?" OK. Moving on. Location!

"Beach?" I ask, hopeful.

"Do we have to do it in the United States? I don't really want to do it there." OK. Moving on. Future ideas!

"We could buy a house and—"

"I don't want to ever buy a house again."

". . . We could travel for a while longer and then begin thinking about starting a family and—"

"I don't want kids."

Everything we want is different. The wedding we envision—hell, the futures we envision—are entirely different. Our engagement means needing to talk about these plans—life plans—for our future, but every time we try, our courses veer off in opposite directions. We each speak of futures the other can't imagine living in.

Still, we try for each other. We anchor in Bocas del Toro: surfing and yoga, grocery store and laundry runs, floating bars and postcard beaches. We party hard to ignore the tough truth: these choppy waves are driven by the gathering storm clouds on our horizon.

It's hard to know exactly *what* is happening at the same moment you know *when* something is happening—and happening in the wrong way. You don't have enough information yet, but it's clear that something is slipping into wrongness. When the truth is too hard to vocalize—*I think we're done with each other*—it's easier to act out, and then experience the relationship ooze like magma, searing everything in its path. So, we act out. He starts chain-smoking cigarettes—I protest. I want a land-living future—he protests.

None of this is love. This is self-sabotage serving as a survival mechanism to avoid what inevitably happens when a relationship ends—abandonment.

I flash back to the first night I met him: interested, carefree, wind blowing through his hair, a lover. Over the course of nearly three years, he's become my boyfriend, my lover, my friend, our boat's captain, a confidante, someone I stand by, and someone who stands by me. My fiancé, even.

We had loved each other. He didn't want to sail alone; I had personal wounds that needed healing, self-worth to discover. Maybe that's why we found each other—to work our own missions out, together. And maybe, a little bit, that is love. We made sense at the time, and we didn't need to know why. It just isn't enough wind to propel us forward now. I pack my belongings.

On Tuesday, January 22, 2019, as the sun is going down, I leave *Seas Hope*. Kallan and I are wrong. We both know it. And that's OK. Sometimes it's better to let the sun go down.

Still in Bocas del Toro, I stay with a woman I met only a week before at a birthday celebration for a mutual boat friend. An American, she lives with her fiancé, a Panamanian, and together they run a social media business for the local hostels, surf clubs, and businesses. Between the party where we met and the follow-up coffee date we had the next day, we have known each other for a maximum of five hours.

"Kelly, may I stay on your couch for a few days?" She barely knows me but that isn't a requirement.

"My door is open!" she writes back immediately. *Thank you, Universe ...*

Kallan delivers my bags and me in our weighed-down dinghy to a dinghy dock attached to a bar. I drag myself to Kelly's apartment and up the stairs where I collapse onto her couch. I stare at her white wall. I replay the last three years in my mind:

I met a guy on the internet.

I helped him bring a sinking boat to life.

I rented out my beach condo, got fired from my job, spread my furniture out among my friends, and donated much of what I owned.

I moved onto his boat.

Most of what I own in the world remains on the boat.

We sailed to various countries and countless islands together.

We faced automatic weapons together!

I agreed to marry him.

> Journal entry: *"'Now the tide sinks. Now the trees come to earth; the brisk waves that slap my ribs rock more gently, and my heart rides at anchor, like a sailing-boat whose sails slide slowly down on to the white deck. The game is over. We must go to tea now.'"*
>
> —Virginia Woolf, *The Waves*

I remember when Kallan taught me about salvaging. A boat was actively sinking before our eyes into the shallow water and mud of Panama. The owner of the vessel had been arrested by INTERPOL so when it started sinking, the police let cruisers take what they wanted before dragging it out of the way to become a home for fish and coral. Kallan took some navy-blue cushions. I filmed the sinking—there's something beautiful about ceding to nature. The water rose higher and higher up his legs as he unscrewed stainless steel boat hardware to help others in need.

"The boat will sink, taking everything with it, whether we take the things we need or not," Kallan said. It didn't make sense to let thousands of dollars of valuable stainless steel and electronics go to waste when cruisers needed it. A navigation system sitting on the sea floor doesn't help fish. So, what on the surface appears to be stealing is more like . . . re-purposing.

Could we salvage our relationship?

Is there anything of value left?

Kelly and I debrief over morning coffee, but I have no answer for "what happened?" It's simply a sudden realization that we—together—don't make sense anymore. It's both of us waking up, looking around, and thinking, *I'm in the wrong place.* It's less the magic wearing off and more us stepping into our own desires for a life without each other.

Kallan comes to see me at Kelly's apartment: a salvage mission. He brings me food, and sits with me in the park, but our love has changed. Along the way, something vital stood up and walked out of the room, severing what we'd had before. And that's OK.

Our time has come. We are losing too much, too fast, a fitting juxtaposition to the start of our relationship where we took on too much, too fast. There's nothing to save here—no navy-blue cushions or top-of-the-line navigation systems—nothing that wouldn't be better off on the bottom of the sea. *Seas Hope* must feel the completion, too. Boat parts begin to loosen, pop, crack, and jam. The toilet stops flushing. The water pump decreases its pressure. Windows leak.

On the day our Canadian friends on *Bella Vista* left us, they came to say goodbye because their year of sailing had come to its end. They had a flight booked for home. They left their boat in Panama with a "For Sale" sign on it—full of the pots, pans, and books they had traveled with. They were heading back to Canada with a singular, shared vision for their future—to find jobs and start a family.

Kallan and I know it's our time to say goodbye—to each other; to sailing away from it all. In my journal, I circled a few lines from the poem "Wild Geese" by Mary Oliver, which guide me through this time:

> "You do not have to be good.
> You do not have to walk on your knees
> for a hundred miles through the desert repenting.
> You only have to let the soft animal of your body
> love what it loves."

Expectation: To be good for each other. Reality: He didn't have to be good for me. I didn't have to be good for him. In fact, that was something we both were no longer interested in being for, or to, each other. We only want to be good for ourselves.

Expectation: "If you loved me, you would (fill in the blank with a request for change) for me." Reality: He didn't need to change—he's wonderful. Same goes for me. We only stopped enjoying each other's kind of wonderful.

Expectation: We complete each other. Reality: We were perfect for each other for the time of life meant for that.

This animal body needs amnesty from love expectations I placed on myself, and on him. Our work together is done. I release him from the obligation to complete me.

Waking up to our new realities, it's our turn to say goodbye to our fellow sailing vessels and to make some decisions about our futures, which we now accept will be separate.

"I started this with you; I want to finish it with you," Kallan says, grabbing the handle of one of my suitcases. "Come back to the boat. Let's finish this the way it's meant to be finished. When we get back to the United States, we can go our separate ways." I nod my head. He's right. This is part of my journey: finishing what I started; completing the circuit. I move back onto Seas Hope—to finish what I began. Two weeks. Over one thousand nautical miles of sailing. Then, we'll close everything out.

CHAPTER FIFTEEN

Heading Home

I sit on the stern with Georgia, my closest girlfriend from the last eight months of my life—when I declared friendship back in Bonaire. Since then, we have cooked, surfed, cried, laughed, gotten lost, been found, explored, folded laundry, made kombucha, and shared soaps and glasses of wine together. A cigarette balances between her fingers; the stem of a glass of wine balances between mine. She absorbs the shock of it all.

"I thought you guys were the real deal." The breakup jolt sent ripples out beyond the two of us and our boat. Hearts hurt expanding out for an unknown radius. What had started as whispers was now confirmed news: "Did you hear? Kallan and Sheena on *Seas Hope* are done." How quickly life changes from celebrating our engagement to sighing out the reality behind the dreamy, imagined-up version of it all.

"Are you ready?" She asks.

I know this question isn't just about what was sure to be our tension-filled sail home. She's asking me if I'm ready to let go of boat life, to restart land life without Kallan: to say goodbye, to get a job, to return to the grind, to pay for electricity and water again—*without Kallan*.

"I don't know," I say. I'm not, but is anyone ready for an unexpected explosion and immediate rebuild following? There's always more money one could've saved to prepare for instances such as this, but *love not working* isn't covered by insurance.

"I'll rebuild with what I've got," I say, holding up my two hands and willingness to work.

"You've got a lot." She smiles and drains her wine glass. I watch the city lights flicker on one at a time. I hear the 9:00 p.m.

horn from the fire department, a tradition in Bocas del Toro that reminds the locals they were once legally required to be locked safely in their homes by this time. Today, the parties are just beginning.

"Whatever happens, you'll be fine," my friend says with confidence. "I know. I know you." I shake my head yes. "I'm going to miss you," she says. My throat locks up.

"I'm going to miss you, too."

At the beginning of our sailing life, we'd turn on Jimmy Buffett songs and sing at the tops of our lungs about sandy toes, sons of sailors, cheeseburgers in paradise, and how it's always five o'clock somewhere. Now, life is beginning to feel like the moment Jimmy Buffett must have had when he wrote "A Pirate Looks at Forty." *Never meant to last, never meant to last. . . .*

Calling it a night, Georgia takes her dinghy home, waving to me with a sad face. I walk to the bow of our boat, pour the remainder of my wine into the sea, and scan the night sky for the moon. She's still there, still glowing. I smile.

* * *

Kallan and I wake up. We haven't touched each other since I moved back onto the boat with the mission "to just finish this." It's business now; I'm basically hired crew. We tackle our challenges before heading out: our emergency position-indicating radio beacon (EPIRB) isn't showing up as registered. Our Garmin isn't broadcasting our position. I am locked out of my e-mail account so I can't alert my family of our plans. We have $500 worth of grains and vegetables on board but no appetites. Our passports are stamped to leave the country. We leave our friends of the last eight months—Georgia and Diego, of *Unforgettable 3*, and Andy, of *Wolfpack*. No more spur-of-the-moment dinner parties or happy hours. No more knocks on the hull before a climb aboard. We are leaving Panama and heading to Key West, Florida.

I stare at the dock lines, recalling the first time I untied them years ago with far more hesitation. Today, I don't hesitate. I am a different woman now. I grant myself permission to go home when it's time to go home. And it's time.

I untie the lines and *Seas Hope* begins her journey home.

Journal entries during the sail back to the United States:

Day 1: Leaving Bocas Del Toro (February 12, 2019)

"Once a wave is set in motion, you can't stop it. There is only arrival."

—Chris Ferreira

Light winds of around ten knots directly on our nose. We motor while sautéing onions, garlic, and peppers for chili. We cook for sustenance. Meals are no longer romantic or set to the tunes of Sinatra.

"Are you hungry?"

"I could eat."

Swells run two to three feet high with four to five second periods. We zoom through one-fourth of our downloaded Netflix shows, mostly because we haven't much to say to each other. My body is reacclimating. I rediscover my sea legs and absorb the swell.

Kallan continues smoking cigarettes. He's telling me with every tobacco-laced inhale and exhale that this is who he is, who he's always been, and who he wants to be. Inhale—"I stopped smoking for you." Exhale—"I never actually wanted to." I get that. I appreciate what he's done for me. My manufactured idea of him lived so differently in my head. It's far easier to love the imagined person than it is to accept who is right in front of you. And it's infuriating because it's impossible to hold that person accountable for your conjured-up version of them: it's simply never who they were.

Night shift—I'm pulling shells off peanuts and chucking them overboard, and the moon is here. Moon, you show up every day with your presence, your light, your wisdom, and your acceptance. You've watched me fail and succeed, fight and let go, expand and contract, and you accept me in every phase, form, and state. You aren't waiting for me to change anything; you just give me space and light to do it—if and when I want. That is love. That is acceptance. That is knowing you can't control someone else's journey.

She is silent. I can feel her smiling.

Day 2: Leaving Lintón Bay Marina (February 12 and 13, 2019)

We pull into Lintón Bay Marina, the anchorage where we once moored for a month during rainy season—the anchorage with the jungle-edge gas station. We intend to spend the night there to download more Netflix films and rest before our weeklong jump, but everything feels abandoned and eerie. Remnants of our old relationship hang over us like clouds. We aren't that couple anymore.

The place itself looks exhausted and dried out. This was the anchorage we came home to after we agreed to get married. If tumbleweeds could bounce across water, I'd expect to see one. All of our boating friends have left—moved on. It feels wrong to be here. We decide to pass through and not even stop. We buy diesel, two Snickers bars, and a six-pack of beer. We wave to the woman who's still there, smoking, waiting for someone to see her.

Day 3: Heading offshore, Caribbean Sea (February 13 and 14, 2019)

Our mainsail rips. We attempt to save it with sail tape, but the wind doesn't care what we try to do and rips it further. We reef down but can no longer get full power from the sail. We're forced to travel slower—exactly what any couple waiting for their official end wants. We make do, working together as a team, seamlessly moving through our duties and shifts.

Valentine's Day: Kallan melts down chocolate chips into the shape of a heart he crafted with tinfoil while I was sleeping. He presents it to me with a face of appreciation for all we've done together, and with a face knowing we won't be looking forward to future Valentine's Days. It makes me smile. I am thankful for all we've done together. We finish all of our Netflix downloads and dig into a reserve hard drive full of downloaded movies given to us by sailors we've met along the way. I break off and swallow pieces of the chocolate heart.

Day 4: Offshore, halfway to Cayman Islands (February 15 and 16, 2019)

Kallan shifts around our shoes, backup water containers, and the extra tubing in our storage hatch. "—Fuck!" We're out of oil and there's zero chance of Amazon delivering engine oil 208 miles offshore from Nicaragua. Since we're a sailboat, we technically don't need to use the engines—the wind can push us. But we've been using them to quicken our speed when the wind is low or nonexistent, plus the wind is still on our nose and our mainsail is compromised. Kallan calculates how much engine-running time we have left. Not much, apparently.

Tonight, we'll make fried rice.

Day 5: Somewhere really far offshore (What day is it?)

A binge day. We watch three movies, pausing only between the first and second to pee and to reheat yesterday's fried rice. We pay the price because we both get tired at the same time but still have to power through night watch.

Time is passing slowly in waves, in nautical miles, in all of the conversations we aren't having. "Tortey," our turtle (female, it turns out—hence the name change from Jhon Guna), climbs around in the box we made for her. She takes spills anytime a large wave tosses us with more power than expected.

Day 6: Offshore, confused seas

The waves are inconsistent. We're going nowhere.

"This sea doesn't know who she is, who she wants to be, where she's going, or what she wants to achieve when she gets there," I say. Kallan shrugs.

"She just wants to stay young."

Day 7: Arrival at Grand Cayman (February 19, 2019, 4:30 a.m.)

I wake up to the sound of the Grand Cayman Port Authority clearing our entrance. Rubbing my eyes awake, I squint to see the lights of the city in the distance. We have made it to our halfway point. We will stay here for a while. Buy engine oil.

It's our last island together. We can—for a last time—sneak into hot tubs and drink overpriced cocktails and hold stingrays and zoom around in our dinghy together. And this we do for days and days until we realize: we can't avoid what's next. We prepare *Seas Hope* and our hearts for our next stop: America: the end of us.

Day 1: Leaving Grand Cayman (February 26 and 27)[12]

I sit with my legs dangling off the edge of a concrete seawall in Grand Cayman Island. A woman in her sixties waits by my side for her husband to lug back the shopping carts we had dragged across the busy highway to the edge of the water where our dinghies sit.

"We filled up our 401(k)s and we're just trying to get by on that 'til the end," she says. "You, you're in your thirties, so you'll have to return to work, but how incredible that you took this time while you're young," she says.

---

12. The days always restart with every new land entry and land exit.

"A lot of people think we messed up big-time," I say, watching the seaweed swirl in the water. "We have very little money left."

"Are you any more poor than you would be on land?" she asks. "Look," she begins, shifting her body to look me straight in the eyes. "There are problems you have and then there are problems you think you have. There's discomfort in having no challenges. There's boredom of paradise. There's debt and illness whether you're walking on water or land. Sometimes, land feels too hard. Sometimes, water feels too soft. It's the nature of things and we adjust. And you'll continue to do just that." I smile. She's right. I know this.

"And as far as money goes, we're supposed to die with no money! Remember that." She scoots her body off the edge of the seawall into her dinghy. "Good luck!"

I am ready for the life unfolding in front me. Kallan finishes securing the last of the groceries.

"You ready?" I jump into our dinghy and yank the engine into a roar. We pour wine into tumblers, and zoom around the island. When we expect nothing from each other—when we grant each other the freedom—we have fun.

Tomorrow, I'll start my goodbyes.

Day 2: Nearing Cuba

To the moon . . .

4:46:02 a.m. I catch a light off in the distance. It's a tanker speeding in our direction. I run outside to change our course but find, to my surprise, it is you, moon. We are headed home, and I think you know this. I am returning home. Do I leave you out here?

I have seen you in many forms:
Large, overflowing, pregnant, heavy.
Small, withered, a shred, a shard, a splinter.
Awkward, misshapen, uneven.
Bold, solitary, confident, and hiding.

Hovering, anxious, blood red.

I have watched you move across the sky and around our boat.

I have witnessed my body react to you. My breasts become full and heavy each month as you do. My blood releases just as you're done being full and ready to start over.

My mother sees her mother in you.

Thank you for lighting the pathways back to me.

Day 3: Rounding Cuba (February 28, 2019)

To the sun. . .

Before you're even seen, you change everything around you. You set the stage of the new day, bringing subtle and delicate shifts of color. A second passes and something is different here. Deep black becomes deep navy and then deep grape. You morph us all.

I used to fear you. So much so, that I'd pay for *spray tans*. I was told you'd bring burns, boils, and blisters, and you did, for a while. I had no trust that you could bring me anything but turmoil and cancer. You would be the reason pieces of my body would have to be cut away. But I started watching you through the eyes of a plant—in the way the palm trees and sunflowers see you. They are unafraid to lean toward you. I wanted to seek you, too.

I began by greeting you each morning with my bare skin. I'd sit before you naked, willing to be touched and warmed by you. At the beginning, you are cool; your rays do not bring heat. I feel you crawl up my body, missing nothing, a rising bath of light. As time passes, you heat up and I feel your confidence grow. My freckles rise to meet you deep within my skin. I sit, unprotected from you, for half an hour. Later, when you're boiling, I meet you again. This time I shade myself from your power. You have no idea how unrelenting you are. Vegetables burst. Animals hide under the shelter of a tree or rock.

There are days when I avoid you. I walk on the sides of the streets where the roofs of buildings block you out. I hang up towels or pillow covers or blankets to keep you out . . . but you always find a sliver of an opening and pour yourself through.

Still, I am sad when you start to leave. In the span of twenty-four hours, my feelings for you follow a spectrum, starting with muted appreciation; then growing louder and more intense—rising to anger, frustration, irritation, and rage, and culminating in a sense of abandonment. I'm going home now, where my life will revolve less around you. But it has been so nice getting to know you. I'm glad we're friends now.

Day 4: Pointing toward Key West (March 1, 2019)

To the sea . . .

To know you in this way has changed me: meeting you where you live, coming out to you and not just knowing your edges. Watching you swell in reaction to the tides and wind, then soothe again—you love both extremes and every day in-between. You carry me, spray me, play with me. You teach me to pay attention. You require of me patience and belief that the waves will eventually arrive—that I will eventually arrive. You tamp down no emotions: if you want to rage, you rage; if you want to weep, you weep; if you want to be peaceful, you rest. I love this about you. It's wildly refreshing to behold. Thank you.

I know for the rest of my life I will close my eyes and see you as I do right now—infinite, hypnotic, ungovernable.

Day 5: March 2, 2019

To Kallan . . .

Our togetherness—alone out here on this open ocean—I will always cherish. The trust—our *lives*—that we placed in the other's hands. I'll remember the evenings, hands clasped, kissing until the sun went away. I'll replay the mornings, you tracing the outline of my fingers, welcoming me back from sleep.

"Hi," you'd say. "I missed you while you were sleeping."

I want you to know nothing soured—we just ripened until we were finished. And we enjoyed the fruit while it was with us: basking in what little we did know, and how much we didn't.

Thank you for being here with me. For these chapters of our lives.

It's been enormously fun.

Day 6: March 3, 2019

The Gulf Stream: We meet again. We were hoping you would help us along, but we're wondering if you're working against us. Both engines are on. The sails are up. And yet it feels like we aren't moving. Days and days we have been here. . . .

Day 7: Arrival at Key West, Florida (March 4, 2019)

"Welcome back to the United States," the border patrol says. "You're home." I run to the bow and cry for hours until I fall asleep. Tears and snot run from my face and fall through the trampoline of *Seas Hope* into the saltwater below.

You're home.
This is the end.
This is finished.

March 5, 2019:

He's told me *not to hurry*. He's told me, *Maybe we can make it work.* We can't. The realizations we've both had are too true to ignore.

The plan is for me to leave. We made it safely back to the United States, and now we're at the part where it's time to go our separate ways. It's painful to know we imagined each other up: he imagined up a *me,* and I imagined up a *him,* and those two imaginary people, under the influence of sand-swept beaches and rum, loved each other. And it was good, but it was fantasy. And how inhuman to want someone to live and love in ways inauthentic to who they are. What a stripped-down version of love—all of the meat is gone. We loved in the way we understood love at the time, and our story needed to stay there to work, but it couldn't. We couldn't.

I pack my belongings.

"I feel sad," he says.

"Me too."

We give ourselves permission to be sad, even when leaving is what's right.

March 7, 2019

The slow drip-drip-drip of my leaving is crushing. We can't speed it up because arrangements have to be made. When a grown adult woman who has been out of the country for nearly two years re-enters with an expired driver's license, $30 in her checking account, and no place to live—it takes a few phone calls. It's hard to be near each other anymore without tears and doors slamming shut in our hearts. Everything hurts. When he pours my morning coffee, I can't help but think: *This the last coffee you'll pour me.* His heart is broken and so is mine—there's no one to blame here. It's just done. While packing up my pots and pans he says, "I am ready to let you go."

I cry. My legs crumble and I sit on the floor to let my body weep. I flash back to our conversation in his kitchen three years ago: "I'm doing this with or without you." He lifts me off the floor and says, "Let's go shower. We need to reset." Holding open the shower door at the marina, he asks, "Do you want to share?" I nod and we walk into the shower room at the marina together.

Lock.

He undresses me and gently directs my body under the shower. The hot water slides down my hair, my face, over my stinging eyes, slipping down my cheeks where it merges with salted tears, makes its way down my chest, my abdomen, and to my feet. It feels good, as land showers do.

He undresses, enters the shower with me, and flips the shampoo bottle over. Shampoo piles up in his hand and he lovingly washes my hair. I close my eyes and I'm back to our waterfall shower hidden by the jungle. *There is so much love here, even if it's not the kind that works forever.* As he makes circular motions, hands deep within my hair, he kisses my forehead.

I am thankful for him. He slowly tilts my head back into the water and pushes the soap backward and it falls away. He washes my body, his hands tenderly caring for me.

What we did together was good.

The shower ends.

It's time I go, even with the details not hammered out.

I finish packing my belongings, smelling of soap. It takes three dinghy rides to transfer all my bags from the boat to land. On each of those dinghy rides, we are afraid the load is too heavy, so we travel slowly. We unload each round into a fellow sailor's borrowed truck. We had only just met him, but he had said, "Shit man, here's the keys," when we told him what was happening. We get to the final round and know I have to say goodbye to this boat. I look around *Seas Hope.*

"Seas . . ." (her nickname), I say, through cries. "I remember when I first met you and I didn't want to spend time with you. I thought you were covered in mold and stinky and sinking. And you were, but I was mean to you, and I'm sorry. I love you now. You kept me safe out there. I'm sorry about the beginning."

"She loves you, too," Kallan says coming up behind me. He squeezes my hand. I sigh and for the last time, step off *Seas Hope,* the boat who showed me the world and helped me discover who I am and what I'm capable of.

At the dinghy dock, I lean down and touch our little blue dinghy. In the sailing world, your dinghy is your car—your ticket from sea to shore and back again. I remember traveling to Maryland to buy her, painting her the color blue, learning how to start her engine, how to steer, learning how to step on and off of her in choppy waves. I remember days when we would zoom around together for the simple delight of feeling the world rush by.

"Goodbye, dinghy. I love you, too."

And then I leave. I walk away from the dock and get into the borrowed truck that will carry me away from *Seas Hope,* from dinghy, ocean living, and from our travels together.

Kallan drives with me until we reach the first location with an available rental car. We pick up a white Ford Taurus—under his name because . . . expired license—and shift my belongings from the truck into the car in a Starbucks parking lot. Kallan will return to *Seas Hope* in Key West; I will drive home to Virginia.

"Go ahead. Get in and adjust your mirrors," Kallan says. "and then . . ."

I am shaking.

". . . We can open the door again."

I am stalling.

I need to go to the bathroom.

Should I buy a coffee?

I need a snack.

I am stalling.

I adjust my mirrors, slowly, though the tears in my eyes defeat any help the mirrors might provide.

"How do you want this to go?" I ask before opening the door again. Kallan forces a smile.

"I'm thinking: kisses, hugs, smiles, an ass squeeze—how does that sound?"

I laugh . . . a little. I remember the very first time I ever spoke to Kallan. I was in a car, talking to him through a rolled-down window just like this.

Open door.
Get out of the car.
Kisses.
Hugs.
Smiles.
Ass squeeze.
Tears.

I say only three things: "I love you so much. Thank you so much. We did good." He holds me and repeats the same things. I let go.

I settle into the car, look over at our turtle in a box in my passenger seat, and I turn the key. I haven't driven a car in years. But it's time to go. This soul journey, complete; I am rewired, returned to me, and renewed as me—stronger than I was before, even in a broken state.

In my rearview mirror, I watch him walk back to the truck. I blow him two kisses. I hesitate at the stop sign. I watch him pull out a cigarette . . . and then I drive away. As I'm speeding down the highway, I catch a glimpse—the moon, unafraid to glow, unafraid to go dark, loving all the while. *You're alive. You're alive. You're alive!*

Acknowledgements

This book started as notes scribbled in my journal beginning in 2016. From there, those notes made their way into a laptop, which the ocean's salted air corroded from the inside out. Transferred, again, to a new computer, the notes traveled with me nautical mile by nautical mile. Eventually, they made their way to the top of the Rocky Mountains, where I completed version one of the book you hold in your hands.

None of these pages would have been seen without . . .

Kallan, who showed up in my life unexpectedly with a grand idea. Who provided me this opportunity of free-range, open-ended travel. Who gave me time and space to jot down notes so that I wouldn't forget a memory. Who inevitably opened up my tightly closed world and understanding.

To my husband, Stephen, who followed my sailing journey on social media, quietly watching. After leaving the boat, I came home with nothing but notes and the intent to write this book, but I had a land life to rebuild first. He cheered me on through all of it. We eventually became in-person friends, started dating, fell deeply in love, then eloped on a mountain in Nicaragua two weeks before the world shut down for COVID-19. The whole while, he's given me space and time to craft this manuscript: a love story that predates him. His tireless love and belief in me kept me going even after the birth of our children, when finding time to write meant him taking on solo parenting. I adore him, and I cherish his belief in me and this book.

To my children, Arlo and Maeve, who taught me how to harness all of the power I felt out in the middle of the ocean and pour that into parenting a wild and free spirit. You change everything.

Neal Petersen and his wife, Darlene, who I met in Colombia, our boats anchored near each other, and with whom I spent many nights dining debating the world's challenges. They led me to Dave Bricker.

To Dave Bricker, my first editor, who bravely responded to my desperate: "I wrote a book but . . . help?" For three years, Dave and I sent this manuscript back and forth, and each time Dave's edits made it stronger and stronger. He was the first person—even before me—to believe in this book. He didn't give up on it on the days that I long had. We began this manuscript as strangers, and ended up as dear friends.

To Jenny DeBell, my second editor, who made this manuscript fly, filling it with life and giving it the wings it needed while guiding me to become a better writer.

To Annie Tobey, my third editor, who caught important details I missed that, when added, completed the story.

To Brandylane Publishers, who picked up my somewhat chaotic collection of notes from the sea and connected me with the perfect people to polish them up for readers.

To my mother, Angela Layne, who struggled so hard with my going sailing, but found it in herself to let her baby go out to sea. Who learned how to text to our satellite phone and then texted me often to check in. Who fought cancer—without me present—and *won*. And, lastly, who served as childcare provider and cheerleader throughout this writing process.

To my father, Christy Jeffers; growing up watching you race cars taught me that bravery and adventure are always worth it.

To my grandfather, Fred R. Skaggs, whom, I believe, my writing talent comes from. He has published many books and taught me to work hard and, always, to show up for myself.

To my aunt Beth and uncle John—the very first people to throw me into large oncoming waves with "Survive!" as the main instruction. Thank you for providing me opportunities to find my courage, and then supporting me as I "survive" my way through.

To the guardian angels who appear in this story. I can't possibly remember each of you who touched my memories and thus my life, but I'll try: Jenn and Mike; Janice and David; Suzie; Brad; Max; Marc; Don and Dierdre "D" Wogaman (*Southern Cross*); Georgia and Diego (*Unforgettable 3*); Steve and Ashley (*Bella Vis-*

ta); Anneli and Nils (*Walkabout*); Andy (*Wolfpack*); Kelly, Nick, and their dog, Arthur (*Sailing Satori*); Mark and Jennifer Prince (*Sailing Lunasea*); Alexis and Kareena Gil (*Valhalla*); Yara and Paulo; Anne-Marie and Tom (*Dagny T*); Ruth; Grace and Derek Rupe (*Captineer*); Sallianne and Douglas Whitman (*Olive Oyl*); Heather and Nathaniel Atwater (*Moonshine*); Julie, Mark, and their daughters, Heidi, Lucy, and Sally (*Love and Luck*); Kathy Belanger-Barber; the Norstrand family; Kelly and Juan Pintos; John and Julie King (*Myla*); Kristen Brush; Camila De Conto (*Sailing Songster*); and Deni and Mike Karpowich, who gave me shelter after I left the boat.

To the beta readers who stuck with me along the way: Madde Vachon, Aíne Norris, Jessi Coble, and Alicia Gerrits. You are brave, caring souls.

To the multiple journals, laptops, cell phones, and iPads I went through—since the saltwater kept actively eating them all away—you all collected images, notes, charts, voice messages, and quotes in order for this book to happen. Thank you for transferring so flawlessly to each new device.

And, lastly, to the members of Women Who Sail—the group of mentors who cultivated me until they knew they had a new sailor on their hands.

About the Author

Sheena Jeffers, MSEd, is a writer, mother, certified wellness coach, doula, and yoga and dance instructor from Virginia. Her work has appeared in the *Richmond Times-Dispatch,* the *Washington Examiner, Waterborne Magazine,* the *Scuttlebutt Sailing News*, and the anthology, *Facing Fear Head On: True Stories from Women on the Water.*

She has been featured on *TODAY*.com, the *Inspired Women Podcast,* the *Roanoke Times*, and in 2016 she was awarded "Millennial on the Move" by *CoVaBiz Mag*. During her travels, she was the host of podcasts *Breathe Full* and *Seas Life for Good*, as well as the producer of a sailing YouTube channel that gathered over ten thousand engaged followers.

Today, Sheena is loving her full days as a mother living by a river, who keeps her lifelong flame for ballet and contemporary dance ablaze, and who, in times of trouble, always remembers to consult the moon.

Printed in the USA
CPSIA information can be obtained
at www.ICGtesting.com
LVHW040615310524
781622LV00008B/9